Mizora: A Pro

by

Mary E. Bradley

The Echo Library 2009

Published by

The Echo Library

Echo Library
131 High St.
Teddington
Middlesex TW11 8HH

www.echo-library.com

Please report serious faults in the text to complaints@echo-library.com

ISBN 978-1-40685-127-4

MIZORA:
A PROPHECY.
A MSS. FOUND AMONG THE PRIVATE PAPERS OF THE PRINCESS VERA ZAROVITCH;

Being a true and faithful account of her Journey to the Interior of the Earth, with a careful description of the Country and its Inhabitants, their Customs, Manners and Government.

WRITTEN BY HERSELF.

NEW YORK:
G. W. Dillingham, Publisher,
Successor to G. W. Carleton & Co.
MDCCCXC.

PREFACE.

The narrative of Vera Zarovitch, published in the *Cincinnati Commercial* in 1880 and 1881, attracted a great deal of attention. It commanded a wide circle of readers, and there was much more said about it than is usual when works of fiction run through a newspaper in weekly installments. Quite a number of persons who are unaccustomed to bestowing consideration upon works of fiction spoke of it, and grew greatly interested in it.

I received many messages about it, and letters of inquiry, and some ladies and gentlemen desired to know the particulars about the production of the story in book form; and were inquisitive about it and the author who kept herself in concealment so closely that even her husband did not know that she was the writer who was making this stir in our limited literary world.

I was myself so much interested in it that it occurred to me to make the suggestion that the story ought to have an extensive sale in book form, and to write to a publisher; but the lady who wrote the work seemed herself a shade indifferent on the subject, and it passed out of my hands and out of my mind.

It is safe to say that it made an impression that was remarkable, and with a larger audience I do not doubt that it would make its mark as an original production wrought out with thoughtful care and literary skill, and take high rank.

Yours very truly,

Murat Halstead.

Nov. 14th, 1889.

PART FIRST   CHAPTER I.

Having little knowledge of rhetorical art, and possessing but a limited imagination, it is only a strong sense of the duty I owe to Science and the progressive minds of the age, that induces me to come before the public in the character of an author. True, I have only a simple narration of facts to deal with, and am, therefore, not expected to present artistic effects, and poetical imagery, nor any of those flights of imagination that are the trial and test of genius.

Yet my task is not a light one. I may fail to satisfy my own mind that the true merits of the wonderful and mysterious people I discovered, have been justly described. I may fail to interest the public; which is the one difficulty most likely to occur, and most to be regretted—not for my own sake, but theirs. It is so hard to get human nature out of the ruts it has moved in for ages. To tear away their present faith, is like undermining their existence. Yet others who come after me will be more aggressive than I. I have this consolation: whatever reception may be given my narrative by the public, I know that it has been written solely for its good. That wonderful civilization I met with in Mizora, I may not be able to more than faintly shadow forth here, yet from it, the present age may form some idea of that grand, that ideal life that is possible for our remote posterity. Again and again has religious enthusiasm pictured a life to be eliminated from the grossness and imperfections of our material existence. The Spirit—the Mind—that mental gift, by or through which we think, reason, and suffer, is by one tragic and awful struggle to free itself from temporal blemishes and difficulties, and become spiritual and perfect. Yet, who, sweeping the limitless fields of space with a telescope, glancing at myriads of worlds that a lifetime could not count, or gazing through a microscope at a tiny world in a drop of water, has dreamed that patient Science and practice could evolve for the living human race, the ideal life of exalted knowledge: the life that I found in Mizora; that Science had made real and practicable. The duty that I owe to truth compels me to acknowledge that I have not been solicited to write this narrative by my friends; nor has it been the pastime of my leisure hours; nor written to amuse an invalid; nor, in fact, for any of those reasons which have prompted so many men and women to write a book. It is, on the contrary, the result of hours of laborious work, undertaken for the sole purpose of benefiting Science and giving encouragement to those progressive minds who have already added their mite of knowledge to the coming future of the race. "We owe a duty to posterity," says Junius in his famous letter to the king. A declaration that ought to be a motto for every schoolroom, and graven above every legislative hall in the world. It should be taught to the child as soon as reason has begun to dawn, and be its guide until age has become its master.

It is my desire not to make this story a personal matter; and for that unavoidable prominence which is given one's own identity in relating personal experiences, an indulgence is craved from whomsoever may peruse these pages.

In order to explain how and why I came to venture upon a journey no other of my sex has ever attempted, I am compelled to make a slight mention of my family and nationality.

I am a Russian: born to a family of nobility, wealth, and political power. Had the natural expectations for my birth and condition been fulfilled, I should have lived, loved, married and died a Russian aristocrat, and been unknown to the next generation—and this narrative would not have been written.

There are some people who seem to have been born for the sole purpose of becoming the playthings of Fate—who are tossed from one condition of life to another without wish or will of their own. Of this class I am an illustration. Had I started out with a resolve to discover the North Pole, I should never have succeeded. But all my hopes, affections, thoughts, and desires were centered in another direction, hence—but my narrative will explain the rest.

The tongue of woman has long been celebrated as an unruly member, and perhaps, in some of the domestic affairs of life, it has been unnecessarily active; yet no one who gives this narrative a perusal, can justly deny that it was the primal cause of the grandest discovery of the age.

I was educated in Paris, where my vacations were frequently spent with an American family who resided there, and with whom my father had formed an intimate friendship. Their house, being in a fashionable quarter of the city and patriotically hospitable, was the frequent resort of many of their countrymen. I unconsciously acquired a knowledge and admiration for their form of government, and some revolutionary opinions in regard to my own.

Had I been guided by policy, I should have kept the latter a secret, but on returning home, at the expiration of my school days, I imprudently gave expression to them in connection with some of the political movements of the Russian Government—and secured its suspicion at once, which, like the virus of some fatal disease, once in the system, would lose its vitality only with my destruction.

While at school, I had become attached to a young and lovely Polish orphan, whose father had been killed at the battle of Grochow when she was an infant in her mother's arms. My love for my friend, and sympathy for her oppressed people, finally drew me into serious trouble and caused my exile from my native land.

I married at the age of twenty the son of my father's dearest friend. Alexis and I were truly attached to each other, and when I gave to my infant the name of my father and witnessed his pride and delight, I thought to my cup of earthly happiness, not one more drop could be added.

A desire to feel the cheering air of a milder climate induced me to pay my Polish friend a visit. During my sojourn with her occurred the anniversary of the tragedy of Grochow, when, according to custom, all who had lost friends in the two dreadful battles that had been fought there, met to offer prayers for their souls. At her request,

I accompanied my friend to witness the ceremonies. To me, a silent and sympathizing spectator, they were impressive and solemn in the extreme. Not less than thirty thousand people were there, weeping and praying on ground hallowed by patriot blood. After the prayers were said, the voice of the multitude rose in a mournful and pathetic chant. It was rudely broken by the appearance of the Russian soldiers.

A scene ensued which memory refuses to forget, and justice forbids me to deny. I saw my friend, with the song of sorrow still trembling on her innocent lips, fall bleeding, dying from the bayonet thrust of a Russian soldier. I clasped the lifeless body in my arms, and in my grief and excitement, poured forth upbraidings against the government of my country which it would never forgive nor condone. I was arrested, tried, and condemned to the mines of Siberia for life.

My father's ancient and princely lineage, my husband's rank, the wealth of both families, all were unavailing in procuring a commutation of my sentence to some less severe punishment. Through bribery, however, the co-operation of one of my jailors was secured, and I escaped in disguise to the frontier.

It was my husband's desire that I proceed immediately to France, where he would soon join me. But we were compelled to accept whatever means chance offered for my escape, and a whaling vessel bound for the Northern Seas was the only thing I could secure passage upon with safety. The captain promised to transfer me to the first southward bound vessel we should meet.

But none came. The slow, monotonous days found me gliding farther and farther from home and love. In the seclusion of my little cabin, my fate was more endurable than the horrors of Siberia could have been, but it was inexpressibly lonesome. On shipboard I sustained the character of a youth, exiled for a political offense, and of a delicate constitution.

It is not necessary to the interest of this narrative to enter into the details of shipwreck and disaster, which befel us in the Northern Seas. Our vessel was caught between ice floes, and we were compelled to abandon her. The small boats were converted into sleds, but in such shape as would make it easy to re-convert them into boats again, should it ever become necessary. We took our march for the nearest Esquimaux settlement, where we were kindly received and tendered the hospitality of their miserable huts. The captain, who had been ill for some time, grew rapidly worse, and in a few days expired. As soon as the approach of death became apparent, he called the crew about him, and requested them to make their way south as soon as possible, and to do all in their power for my health and comfort. He had, he said, been guaranteed a sum of money for my safe conduct to France, sufficient to place his family in independent circumstances, and he desired that his crew should do all in their power to secure it for them.

The next morning I awoke to find myself deserted, the crew having decamped with nearly everything brought from the ship.

Being blessed with strong nerves, I stared my situation bravely in the face, and resolved to make the best of it. I believed it could be only a matter of time when some European or American whaling vessel should rescue me: and I had the resolution to endure, while hope fed the flame.

I at once proceeded to inure myself to the life of the Esquimaux. I habited myself in a suit of reindeer fur, and ate, with compulsory appetite, the raw flesh and fat that form their principal food. Acclimated by birth to the coldest region of the temperate zone, and naturally of a hardy constitution, I found it not so difficult to endure the rigors of the Arctic temperature as I had supposed.

I soon discovered the necessity of being an assistance to my new friends in procuring food, as their hospitality depends largely upon the state of their larder. A compass and a small trunk of instruments belonging to the Captain had been either over-looked or rejected by the crew in their flight. I secured the esteem of the Esquimaux by using the compass to conduct a hunting party in the right direction when a sudden snow-storm had obscured the landmarks by which they guide their course. I cheerfully assumed a share of their hardships, for with these poor children of the North life is a continual struggle with cold and starvation. The long, rough journeys which we frequently took over ice and ridges of snow in quest of animal food, I found monotonously destitute of everything I had experienced in former traveling, except fatigue. The wail of the winds, and the desolate landscape of ice and snow, never varied. The coruscations of the Aurora Borealis sometimes lighted up the dreary waste around us, and the myriad eyes of the firmament shone out with a brighter lustre, as twilight shrank before the gloom of the long Arctic night.

A description of the winter I spent with the Esquimaux can be of little interest to the readers of this narrative. Language cannot convey to those who have dwelt always in comfort the feeling of isolation, the struggle with despair, that was constantly mine. We were often confined to our ice huts for days while the blinding fury of the wind driven snow without made the earth look like chaos. Sometimes I crept to the narrow entrance and looked toward the South with a feeling of homesickness too intense to describe. Away, over leagues of perilous travel, lay everything that was dear or congenial; and how many dreary months, perhaps years, must pass before I could obtain release from associations more dreadful than solitude. It required all the courage I could command to endure it.

The whale-fishing opens about the first week in August, and continues throughout September. As it drew near, the settlement prepared to move farther north, to a locality where they claimed whales could be found in abundance. I cheerfully assisted in the preparations, for to meet some whaling vessel was my only hope of rescue from surroundings that made existence a living death.

The dogs were harnessed to sleds heavily laden with the equipments of an Esquimaux hut. The woman, as well as the men, were burdened with immense packs; and our journey begun. We halted only to rest and sleep. A few hours work furnished us a new house out of the ever present ice. We feasted on raw meat—sometimes a freshly killed deer; after which our journey was resumed.

As near as I could determine, it was close to the 85 deg. north latitude, where we halted on the shore of an open sea. Wild ducks and game were abundant, also fish of an excellent quality. Here, for the first time in many months, I felt the kindly greeting of a mild breeze as it hailed me from the bosom of the water. Vegetation was not profuse nor brilliant, but to my long famished eyes, its dingy hue was delightfully refreshing.

Across this sea I instantly felt a strong desire to sail. I believed it must contain an island of richer vegetation than the shore we occupied. But no one encouraged me or would agree to be my companion. On the contrary, they intimated that I should never return. I believed that they were trying to frighten me into remaining with them, and declared my intention to go alone. Perhaps I might meet in that milder climate some of my own race. My friend smiled, and pointing to the South, said, as he designated an imaginary boundary:

"Across *that* no white man's foot has ever stepped."

So I was alone. My resolution, however, was not shaken. A boat was constructed, and bidding adieu to my humble companions, I launched into an unknown sea.

CHAPTER II.

On and on, and on I rowed until the shore and my late companions were lost in the gloomy distance. On and on, and still on, until fatigued almost to exhaustion; and still, no land. A feeling of uncontrollable lonesomeness took possession of me. Silence reigned supreme. No sound greeted me save the swirl of the gently undulating waters against the boat, and the melancholy dip of the oars. Overhead, the familiar eyes of night were all that pierced the gloom that seemed to hedge me in. My feeling of distress increased when I discovered that my boat had struck a current and was beyond my control. Visions of a cataract and inevitable death instantly shot across my mind. Made passive by intense despair, I laid down in the bottom of the boat, to let myself drift into whatever fate was awaiting me.

I must have lain there many hours before I realized that I was traveling in a circle. The velocity of the current had increased, but not sufficiently to insure immediately destruction. Hope began to revive, and I sat up and looked about me with renewed courage. Directly before me rose a column of mist, so thin that I could see through it, and of the most delicate tint of green. As I gazed, it spread into a curtain that appeared to be suspended in mid-air, and began to sway gently back and forth, as if impelled by a slight breeze, while sparks of fire, like countless swarms of fire-flies, darted through it and blazed out into a thousand brilliant hues and flakes of color that chased one another across and danced merrily up and down with bewildering swiftness. Suddenly it drew together in a single fold, a rope of yellow mist, then instantly shook itself out again as a curtain of rainbows fringed with flame. Myriads of tassels, composed of threads of fire, began to dart hither and thither through it, while the rainbow stripes deepened in hue until they looked like gorgeous ribbons glowing with intensest radiance, yet softened by that delicate misty appearance which is a special quality of all atmospheric color, and which no pencil can paint, nor the most eloquent tongue adequately describe.

The swaying motion continued. Sometimes the curtain approached near enough, apparently, to flaunt its fiery fringe almost within my grasp. It hung one instant in all its marvelous splendor of colors, then suddenly rushed into a compact mass, and shot across the zenith, an arc of crimson fire that lit up the gloomy waters with a weird, unearthly glare. It faded quickly, and appeared to settle upon the water again in a circular wall of amber mist, round which the current was hurrying me with rapidly increasing speed. I saw, with alarm, that the circles were narrowing A whirlpool was my instant conjecture, and I laid myself down in the boat, again expecting every moment to be swept into a seething abyss of waters. The spray dashed into my face as the boat plunged forward with frightful swiftness. A semi-stupor, born of exhaustion and terror, seized me in its merciful embrace.

It must have been many hours that I lay thus. I have a dim recollection of my boat going on and on, its speed gradually decreasing, until I was amazed to perceive that it had ceased its onward motion and was gently rocking on quiet waters. I opened my eyes. A rosy light, like the first blush of a new day, permeated the atmosphere. I sat up and looked about me. A circular wall of pale amber mist rose behind me; the shores of a new and beautiful country stretched before. Toward them, I guided my boat with reviving hope and strength.

I entered a broad river, whose current was from the sea, and let myself drift along its banks in bewildered delight. The sky appeared bluer, and the air balmier than even that of Italy's favored clime. The turf that covered the banks was smooth and fine, like a carpet of rich green velvet. The fragrance of tempting fruit was wafted by the zephyrs from numerous orchards. Birds of bright plumage flitted among the branches, anon breaking forth into wild and exultant melody, as if they rejoiced to be in so favored a clime.

And truly it seemed a land of enchantment. The atmosphere had a peculiar transparency, seemingly to bring out clearly objects at a great distance, yet veiling the far horizon in a haze of gold and purple. Overhead, clouds of the most gorgeous hues, like precious gems converted into vapor, floated in a sky of the serenest azure. The languorous atmosphere, the beauty of the heavens, the inviting shores, produced in me a feeling of contentment not easily described. To add to my senses another enjoyment, my ears were greeted with sounds of sweet music, in which I detected the mingling of human voices.

I wondered if I had really drifted into an enchanted country, such as I had read about in the fairy books of my childhood.

The music grew louder, yet wondrously sweet, and a large pleasure boat, shaped like a fish, glided into view. Its scales glittered like gems as it moved gracefully and noiselessly through the water. Its occupants were all young girls of the highest type of blonde beauty. It was their soft voices, accompanied by some peculiar stringed instruments they carried, that had produced the music I had heard. They appeared to regard me with curiosity, not unmixed with distrust, for their boat swept aside to give me a wide berth.

I uncovered my head, shook down my long black hair, and falling upon my knees, lifted my hands in supplication. My plea was apparently understood, for turning their boat around, they motioned me to follow them. This I did with difficulty, for I was weak, and their boat moved with a swiftness and ease that astonished me. What surprised me most was its lack of noise.

As I watched its beautiful occupants dressed in rich garments, adorned with rare and costly gems, and noted the noiseless, gliding swiftness of their boat, an uncomfortable feeling of mystery began to invade my mind, as though I really had chanced upon enchanted territory.

As we glided along, I began to be impressed by the weird stillness. No sound greeted me from the ripening orchards, save the carol of birds; from the fields came no note of harvest labor. No animals were visible, nor sound of any. No hum of life. All nature lay asleep in voluptuous beauty, veiled in a glorious atmosphere. Everything wore a dreamy look. The breeze had a loving, lingering touch, not unlike to the Indian Summer of North America. But no Indian Summer ever knew that dark green verdure, like the first robe of spring. Wherever the eye turned it met something charming in cloud, or sky, or water, or vegetation. Everything had felt the magical touch of beauty.

On the right, the horizon was bounded by a chain of mountains, that plainly showed their bases above the glowing orchards and verdant landscapes. It impressed me as peculiar, that everything appeared to rise as it gained in distance. At last the pleasure boat halted at a flight of marble steps that touched the water. Ascending these, I gained an eminence where a scene of surpassing beauty and grandeur lay spread before me. Far, far as the eye could follow it, stretched the stately splendor of a mighty city. But all the buildings were detached and surrounded by lawns and shade trees, their white marble and gray granite walls gleaming through the green foliage.

Upon the lawn, directly before us, a number of most beautiful girls had disposed themselves at various occupations. Some were reading, some sketching, and some at various kinds of needlework. I noticed that they were all blondes. I could not determine whether their language possessed a peculiarly soft accent, or whether it was an unusual melody of voice that made their conversation as musical to the ear as the love notes of some amorous wood bird to its mate.

A large building of white marble crowned a slight eminence behind them. Its porticos were supported upon the hands of colossal statues of women, carved out of white marble with exquisite art and beauty. Shade trees of a feathery foliage, like plumes of finest moss, guarded the entrance and afforded homes for brilliant-plumaged birds that flew about the porticos and alighted on the hands and shoulders of the ladies without fear. Some of the trees had a smooth, straight trunk and flat top, bearing a striking resemblance to a Chinese umbrella. On either side of the marble-paved entrance were huge fountains that threw upward a column of water a hundred feet in height, which, dissolving into spray, fell into immense basins of clearest crystal. Below the rim of these basins, but covered with the crystal, as with a delicate film of ice, was a wreath of blood red roses, that looked as though they had just been plucked from the stems and placed there for a temporary ornament. I afterward learned that it was the work of an artist, and durable as granite.

I supposed I had arrived at a female seminary, as not a man, or the suggestion of one, was to be seen. If it were a seminary, it was for the wealth of the land, as house, grounds, adornments, and the ladies' attire were rich and elegant.

I stood apart from the groups of beautiful creatures like the genus of another race, enveloped in garments of fur that had seen much service. I presented a marked contrast. The evident culture, refinement, and gentleness of the ladies, banished any fear I might have entertained as to the treatment I should receive. But a singular silence that pervaded everything impressed me painfully. I stood upon the uplifted verge of an immense city, but from its broad streets came no sound of traffic, no rattle of wheels, no hum of life. Its marble homes of opulence shone white and grand through mossy foliage; from innumerable parks the fountains sparkled and statues gleamed like rare gems upon a costly robe; but over all a silence, as of death, reigned unbroken. The awe and the mystery of it pressed heavily upon my spirit, but I could not refuse to obey when a lady stepped out of the group, that had doubtless been discussing me, and motioned me to follow her.

She led me through the main entrance into a lofty hall that extended through the entire building, and consisted of a number of grand arches representing scenes in high relief of the finest sculpture. We entered a magnificent salon, where a large assembly of ladies regarded me with unmistakable astonishment. Every one of them was a blonde. I was presented to one, whom I instantly took to be the Lady Superior of the College, for I had now settled it in my mind that I was in a female seminary, albeit one of unheard of luxury in its appointments.

The lady had a remarkable majesty of demeanor, and a noble countenance. Her hair was white with age, but over her features, the rosy bloom of youth still lingered, as if loth to depart. She looked at me kindly and critically, but not with as much surprise as the others had evinced. I may here remark that I am a brunette. My guide, having apparently received some instruction in regard to me, led me upstairs into a private apartment. She placed before me a complete outfit of female wearing apparel, and informed me by signs that I was to put it on. She then retired. The apartment was sumptuously furnished in two colors—amber and lazulite. A bath-room adjoining had a beautiful porcelain tank with scented water, that produced a delightful feeling of exhilaration.

Having donned my new attire, I descended the stairs and met my guide, who conducted me into a spacious dining-room. The walls were adorned with paintings, principally of fruit and flowers. A large and superb picture of a sylvan dell in the side of a rock, was one exception. Its deep, cool shadows, and the pellucid water, which a wandering sunbeam accidentally revealed, were strikingly realistic. Nearly all of the pictures were upon panels of crystal that were set in the wall. The light shining through them gave them an exceedingly natural effect. One picture that I especially admired, was of a grape vine twining around the body and trunk of an old tree. It was inside of the crystal panel, and looked so natural that I imagined I could see its leaves and tendrils sway in the wind. The occupants of the dining-room were all ladies, and again I noted the fact that they were all blondes: beautiful, graceful, courteous, and with voices softer and sweeter than the strains of an eolian harp.

The table, in its arrangement and decoration, was the most beautiful one I had ever seen. The white linen cloth resembled brocaded satin. The knives and forks were gold, with handles of solid amber. The dishes were of the finest porcelain. Some of them, particularly the fruit stands, looked as though composed of hoar frost. Many of the fruit stands were of gold filigree work. They attracted my notice at once, not so much on account of the exquisite workmanship and unique design of the dishes, as the wonderful fruit they contained. One stand, that resembled a huge African lily in design, contained several varieties of plums, as large as hen's eggs, and transparent. They were yellow, blue and red. The centre of the table was occupied by a fruit stand of larger size than the others. It looked like a boat of sea foam fringed with gold moss. Over its outer edge hung clusters of grapes of a rich wine color, and clear as amethysts. The second row looked like globes of honey, the next were of a pale, rose color, and the top of the pyramid was composed of white ones, the color and transparency of dew.

The fruit looked so beautiful. I thought it would be a sacrilege to destroy the charm it had for the eye; but when I saw it removed by pink tipped fingers, whose beauty no art could represent, and saw it disappear within such tempting lips. I thought the feaster worthy of the feast. Fruit appeared to be the principal part of their diet, and was served in its natural state. I was, however, supplied with something that resembled beefsteak of a very fine quality. I afterward learned that it was chemically prepared meat. At the close of the meal, a cup was handed me that looked like the half of a soap bubble with all its iridescent beauty sparkling and glancing in the light. It contained a beverage that resembled chocolate, but whose flavor could not have been surpassed by the fabled nectar of the gods.

CHAPTER III.

I have been thus explicit in detailing the circumstances of my entrance into the land of Mizora, or, in other words, the interior of the earth, lest some incredulous person might doubt the veracity of this narrative.

It does seem a little astonishing that a woman should have fallen by accident, and without intention or desire, upon a discovery that explorers and scientists had for years searched for in vain. But such was the fact, and, in generosity, I have endeavored to make my accident as serviceable to the world in general, and Science in particular, as I could, by taking observations of the country, its climate and products, and especially its people.

I met with the greatest difficulty in acquiring their language. Accustomed to the harsh dialect of the North, my voice was almost intractable in obtaining their melodious accentuation. It was, therefore, many months before I mastered the difficulty sufficiently to converse without embarrassment, or to make myself clearly understood. The construction of their language was simple and easily understood, and in a short time I was able to read it with ease, and to listen to it with enjoyment. Yet, before this was accomplished, I had mingled among them for months, listening to a musical jargon of conversation, that I could neither participate in, nor understand. All that I could therefore discover about them during this time, was by observation. This soon taught me that I was not in a seminary—in our acceptance of the term—but in a College of Experimental Science. The ladies—girls I had supposed them to be—were, in fact, women and mothers, and had reached an age that with us would be associated with decrepitude, wrinkles and imbecility. They were all practical chemists, and their work was the preparation of food from the elements. No wonder that they possessed the suppleness and bloom of eternal youth, when the earthy matter and impurities that are ever present in our food, were unknown to theirs.

I also discovered that they obtained rain artificially when needed, by discharging vast quantities of electricity in the air. I discovered that they kept no cattle, nor animals of any kind for food or labor. I observed a universal practice of outdoor exercising; the aim seeming to be to develop the greatest capacity of lung or muscle. It was astonishing the amount of air a Mizora lady could draw into her lungs. They called it their brain stimulant, and said that their faculties were more active after such exercise. In my country, a cup of strong coffee, or some other agreeable beverage, is usually taken into the stomach to invigorate or excite the mind.

One thing I remarked as unusual among a people of such cultured taste, and that was the size of the ladies' waists. Of all that I measured not one was less than thirty inches in circumference, and it was rare to meet with one that small. At first I thought a waist that tapered from the arm pits would be an added beauty, if only these ladies would be taught how to acquire it. But I lived long enough among them to look upon a tapering waist as a disgusting deformity. They considered a large waist a mark of beauty, as it gave a greater capacity of lung power; and they laid the greatest stress upon the size and health of the lungs. One little lady, not above five feet in height, I saw draw into her lungs two hundred and twenty-five cubic inches of air, and smile proudly when she accomplished it. I measured five feet and five inches in height, and with the greatest effort I could not make my lungs receive more than two hundred cubic inches of air. In my own country I had been called an unusually robust girl, and knew, by comparison, that I had a much larger and fuller chest than the average among women.

I noticed with greater surprise than anything else had excited in me, the marked absence of men. I wandered about the magnificent building without hindrance or surveillance. There was not a lock or bolt on any door in it. I frequented a vast gallery filled with paintings and statues of women, noble looking, beautiful women, but still— nothing but women. The fact that they were all blondes, singular as it might appear, did not so much impress me. Strangers came and went, but among the multitude of faces I met, I never saw a man's.

In my own country I had been accustomed to regard man as a vital necessity. He occupied all governmental offices, and was the arbitrator of domestic life. It seemed, therefore, impossible to me for a country or government to survive without his assistance and advice. Besides, it was a country over which the heart of any man must yearn, however insensible he might be to beauty or female loveliness. Wealth was everywhere and abundant. The climate as delightful as the most fastidious could desire. The products of the orchards and gardens surpassed description. Bread came from the laboratory, and not from the soil by the sweat of the brow. Toil was unknown; the toil that we know, menial, degrading and harassing. Science had been the magician that had done away all that. Science, so formidable and austere to our untutored minds, had been gracious to these fair beings and opened the door to nature's most occult secrets. The beauty of those women it is not in my power to describe. The Greeks, in their highest art, never rivalled it, for here was a beauty of mind that no art can represent. They enhanced their physical charms with attractive costumes, often of extreme elegance. They wore gems that flashed a fortune as they passed. The rarest was of a pale rose color, translucent as the clearest water, and of a brilliancy exceeding the finest diamond. Their voices, in song, could only be equaled by a celestial choir. No dryad queen ever floated through the leafy aisles of her forest with more grace than they displayed in every movement. And all this was for feminine eyes alone—and they of the most enchanting loveliness.

Among all the women that I met during my stay in Mizora—comprising a period of fifteen years—I saw not one homely face or ungraceful form. In my own land the voice of flattery had whispered in my ear praises of face and figure, but I felt ill-formed and uncouth beside the perfect symmetry and grace of these lovely beings. Their chief beauty appeared in a mobility of expression. It was the divine fire of Thought that illumined every feature, which, while gazing upon the Aphrodite of Praxitiles, we must think was all that the matchless marble lacked. Emotion passed over their features like ripples over a stream. Their eyes were limpid wells of loveliness, where every impulse of their natures were betrayed without reserve.

"It would be a paradise for man."

I made this observation to myself, and as secretly would I propound the question:

"Why is he not here in lordly possession?"

In *my* world man was regarded, or he had made himself regarded, as a superior being. He had constituted himself the Government, the Law, Judge, Jury and Executioner. He doled out reward or punishment as his conscience or judgment dictated. He was active and belligerent always in obtaining and keeping every good thing for himself. He was indispensable. Yet here was a nation of fair, exceedingly fair women doing without him, and practising the arts and sciences far beyond the imagined pale of human knowledge and skill.

Of their progress in science I will give some accounts hereafter.

It is impossible to describe the feeling that took possession of me as months rolled by, and I saw the active employments of a prosperous people move smoothly and quietly along in the absence of masculine intelligence and wisdom. Cut off from all inquiry by my ignorance of their language, the singular absence of the male sex began to prey upon my imagination as a mystery. The more so after visiting a town at some distance, composed exclusively of schools and colleges for the youth of the country. Here I saw hundreds of children—*and all of them were girls.* Is it to be wondered at that the first inquiry I made, was:

"Where are the men?"

CHAPTER IV.

To facilitate my progress in the language of Mizora I was sent to their National College. It was the greatest favor they could have conferred upon me, as it opened to me a wide field of knowledge. Their educational system was a peculiar one, and, as it was the chief interest of the country. I shall describe it before proceeding farther with this narrative.

All institutions for instruction were public, as were, also, the books and other accessories. The State was the beneficent mother who furnished everything, and required of her children only their time and application. Each pupil was compelled to attain a certain degree of excellence that I thought unreasonably high, after which she selected the science or vocation she felt most competent to master, and to that she then devoted herself.

The salaries of teachers were larger than those of any other public position. The Principal of the National College had an income that exceeded any royal one I had ever heard of; but, as education was the paramount interest of Mizora, I was not surprised at it. Their desire was to secure the finest talent for educational purposes, and as the highest honors and emoluments belonged to such a position, it could not be otherwise. To be a teacher in Mizora was to be a person of consequence. They were its aristocracy.

Every State had a free college provided for out of the State funds. In these colleges every department of Science, Art, or Mechanics was furnished with all the facilities for thorough instruction. All the expenses of a pupil, including board, clothing, and the necessary traveling fares, were defrayed by the State. I may here remark that all railroads are owned and controlled by the General Government. The rates of transportation were fixed by law, and were uniform throughout the country.

The National College which I entered belonged to the General Government. Here was taught the highest attainments in the arts and sciences, and all industries practised in Mizora. It contained the very cream of learning. There the scientist, the philosopher and inventor found the means and appliances for study and investigation. There the artist and sculptor had their finest work, and often their studios. The principals and subordinate teachers and assistants were elected by popular vote. The State Colleges were free to those of another State who might desire to enter them, for Mizora was like one vast family. It was regarded as the duty of every citizen to lend all the aid and encouragement in her power to further the enlightenment of others, wisely knowing the benefits of such would accrue to her own and the general good. The National College was open to all applicants, irrespective of age, the only requirements being a previous training to enter upon so high a plane of mental culture. Every allurement was held out to the people to come and drink at the public fountain where the cup was inviting and the waters sweet. "For," said one of the leading instructors to me, "education is the foundation of our moral elevation, our government, our happiness.

Let us relax our efforts, or curtail the means and inducements to become educated, and we relax into ignorance, and end in demoralization. We know the value of free education. It is frequently the case that the greatest minds are of slow development, and manifest in the primary schools no marked ability. They often leave the schools unnoticed; and when time has awakened them to their mental needs, all they have to do is to apply to the college, pass an examination, and be admitted. If not prepared to enter the college, they could again attend the common schools. We realize in its broadest sense the ennobling influence of universal education. The higher the culture of a people, the more secure is their government and happiness. A prosperous people is always an educated one; and the freer the education, the wealthier they become."

The Preceptress of the National College was the leading scientist of the country. Her position was more exalted than any that wealth could have given her. In fact, while wealth had acknowledged advantages, it held a subordinate place in the estimation of the people. I never heard the expression "very wealthy," used as a recommendation of a person. It was always: "*She* is a fine scholar, or mechanic, or artist, or musician. *She* excels in landscape gardening, or domestic work. *She* is a first-class chemist." But never "*She* is rich."

The idea of a Government assuming the responsibility of education, like a parent securing the interest of its children, was all so new to me; and yet, I confessed to myself, the system might prove beneficial to other countries than Mizora. In that world, from whence I had so mysteriously emigrated, education was the privilege only of the rich. And in no country, however enlightened, was there a system of education that would reach all. Charitable institutions were restricted, and benefited only a few. My heart beat with enthusiasm when I thought of the mission before me. And then I reflected that the philosophers of my world were but as children in progress compared to these. Still traveling in grooves that had been worn and fixed for posterity by bygone ages of ignorance and narrow-mindedness, it would require courage and resolution, and more eloquence than I possessed, to persuade them out of these trodden paths. To be considered the privileged class was an active characteristic of human nature. Wealth, and the powerful grip upon the people which the organizations of society and governments gave, made it hereditary. Yet in this country, nothing was hereditary but the prosperity and happiness of the whole people.

It was not a surprise to me that astronomy was an unknown science in Mizora, as neither sun, moon, nor stars were visible there. "The moon's pale beams" never afford material for a blank line in poetry; neither do scientific discussions rage on the formation of Saturn's rings, or the spots on the sun. They knew they occupied a hollow sphere, bounded North and South by impassible oceans. Light was a property of the atmosphere. A circle of burning mist shot forth long streamers of light from the North, and a similar phenomena occurred in the South.

The recitation of my geography lesson would have astonished a pupil from the outer world. They taught that a powerful current of electricity existed in the upper regions of the atmosphere. It was the origin of their atmospheric heat and light, and their change of seasons. The latter appeared to me to coincide with those of the Arctic zone, in one particular. The light of the sun during the Arctic summer is reflected by the atmosphere, and produces that mellow, golden, rapturous light that hangs like a veil of enchantment over the land of Mizora for six months in the year. It was followed by six months of the shifting iridescence of the Aurora Borealis.

As the display of the Aurora Borealis originated, and was most brilliant at what appeared to me to be the terminus of the pole, I believed it was caused by the meeting at that point of the two great electric currents of the earth, the one on its surface, and the one known to the inhabitants of Mizora. The heat produced by the meeting of two such powerful currents of electricity is, undoubtedly, the cause of the open Polar Sea. As the point of meeting is below the vision of the inhabitants of the Arctic regions, they see only the reflection of the Aurora. Its gorgeous, brilliant, indescribable splendor is known only to the inhabitants of Mizora.

At the National College, where it is taught as a regular science, I witnessed the chemical production of bread and a preparation resembling meat. Agriculture in this wonderful land, was a lost art. No one that I questioned had any knowledge of it. It had vanished in the dim past of their barbarism. With the exception of vegetables and fruit, which were raised in luscious perfection, their food came from the elements. A famine among such enlightened people was impossible, and scarcity was unknown. Food for the body and food for the mind were without price. It was owing to this that poverty was unknown to them, as well as disease. The absolute purity of all that they ate preserved an activity of vital power long exceeding our span of life. The length of their year, measured by the two seasons, was the same as ours, but the women who had marked a hundred of them in their lifetime, looked younger and fresher, and were more supple of limb than myself, yet I had barely passed my twenty-second year.

I wrote out a careful description of the processes by which they converted food out of the valueless elements—valueless because of their abundance—and put it carefully away for use in my own country. There drouth, or excessive rainfalls, produced scarcity, and sometimes famine. The struggle of the poor was for food, to the exclusion of all other interests. Many of them knew not what proper and health-giving nourishment was. But here in Mizora, the daintiest morsels came from the chemists laboratory, cheap as the earth under her feet.

I now began to enjoy the advantages of conversation, which added greatly to my happiness and acquirements. I formed an intimate companionship with the daughter of the Preceptress of the National College, and to her was addressed the questions I asked about things that impressed me. She was one of the most beautiful beings that it had been my lot to behold. Her eyes were dark, almost the purplish blue of a pansy, and her hair had a darker tinge than is common in Mizora, as if it had stolen the golden edge of a ripe chestnut. Her beauty was a constant charm to me.

The National College contained a large and well filled gallery. Its pictures and statuary were varied, not confined to historical portraits and busts as was the one at the College of Experimental Science. Yet it possessed a number of portraits of women exclusively of the blonde type. Many of them were ideal in loveliness. This gallery also contained the masterpieces of their most celebrated sculptors. They were all studies of the female form. I am a connoisseur in art, and nothing that I had ever seen before could compare with these matchless marbles, bewitching in every delicate contour, alluring in softness, but grand and majestic in pose and expression.

But I haunted this gallery for other reasons than its artistic attractions. I was searching for the portrait of a man, or something suggesting his presence. I searched in vain. Many of the paintings were on a peculiar transparent substance that gave to the subject a startlingly vivid effect. I afterward learned that they were imperishable, the material being a translucent adamant of their own manufacture. After a picture was painted upon it, another piece of adamant was cemented over it.

Each day, as my acquaintance with the peculiar institutions and character of the inhabitants of Mizora increased, my perplexity and a certain air of mystery about them increased with it. It was impossible for me not to feel for them a high degree of respect, admiration, and affection. They were ever gentle, tender, and kind to solicitude. To accuse them of mystery were a paradox; and yet they *were* a mystery. In conversation, manners and habits, they were frank to singularity. It was just as common an occurrence for a poem to be read and commented on by its author, as to hear it done by another. I have heard a poetess call attention to the beauties of her own production, and receive praise or adverse criticism with the same charming urbanity.

Ambition of the most intense earnestness was a natural characteristic, but was guided by a stern and inflexible justice. Envy and malice were unknown to them. It was, doubtless, owing to their elevated moral character that courts and legal proceedings had become unnecessary. If a discussion arose between parties involving a question of law, they repaired to the Public Library, where the statute books were kept, and looked up the matter themselves, and settled it as the law directed. Should they fail to interpret the law alike, a third party was selected as referee, but accepted no pay.

Indolence was as much a disgrace to them as is the lack of virtue to the women of my country, hence every citizen, no matter how wealthy, had some regular trade, business or profession. I found those occupations we are accustomed to see accepted by the people of inferior birth and breeding, were there filled by women of the highest social rank, refined in manner and frequently of notable intellectual acquirements. It grew, or was the result of the custom of selecting whatever vocation they felt themselves competent to most worthily fill, and as no social favor or ignominy rested on any kind of labor, the whole community of Mizora was one immense family of sisters who knew no distinction of birth or position among themselves.

There were no paupers and no charities, either public or private, to be found in the country. The absence of poverty such as I knew existed in all civilized nations upon the face of the earth, was largely owing to the cheapness of food. But there was one other consideration that bore vitally upon it. The dignity and necessity of labor was early and diligently impressed upon the mind. The Preceptress said to me:

"Mizora is a land of industry. Nature has taught us the duty of work. Had some of us been born with minds fully matured, or did knowledge come to some as old age comes to all, we might think that a portion was intended to live without effort. But we are all born equal, and labor is assigned to all; and the one who seeks labor is wiser than the one who lets labor seek her."

Citizens, I learned, were not restrained from accumulating vast wealth had they the desire and ability to do so, but custom imposed upon them the most honorable processes. If a citizen should be found guilty of questionable business transactions, she suffered banishment to a lonely island and the confiscation of her entire estate, both hereditary and acquired. The property confiscated went to the public schools in the town or city where she resided; but never was permitted to augment salaries. I discovered this in the statute books, but not in the memory of any one living had it been found necessary to inflict such a punishment.

"Our laws," said Wauna, "are simply established legal advice. No law can be so constructed as to fit every case so exactly that a criminal mind could not warp it into a dishonest use. But in a country like ours, where civilization has reached that state of enlightenment that needs no laws, we are simply guided by custom."

The love of splendor and ornament was a pronounced characteristic of these strange people. But where gorgeous colors were used, they were always of rich quality. The humblest homes were exquisitely ornamented, and often displayed a luxury that, with us, would have been considered an evidence of wealth.

They took the greatest delight in their beauty, and were exceedingly careful of it. A lovely face and delicate complexion, they averred, added to one's refinement. The art of applying an artificial bloom and fairness to the skin, which I had often seen practiced in my own country, appeared to be unknown to them. But everything savoring of deception was universally condemned. They made no concealment of the practice they resorted to for preserving their complexions, and so universal and effectual were they, that women who, I was informed, had passed the age allotted to the grandmothers in my country, had the smooth brow and pink bloom of cheek that belongs to a more youthful period of life. There was, however, a distinction between youth and old age. The hair was permitted to whiten, but the delicate complexion of old age, with its exquisite coloring, excited in my mind as much admiration as astonishment.

I cannot explain why I hesitated to press my first inquiry as to where the men were. I had put the question to Wauna one day, but she professed never to have heard of such beings. It silenced me—for a time.

"Perhaps it is some extinct animal," she added, naively. "We have so many new things to study and investigate, that we pay but little attention to ancient history."

I bided my time and put the query in another form.

"Where is your other parent?"

She regarded me with innocent surprise. "You talk strangely. I have but one parent. How could I have any more?"

"You ought to have two."

She laughed merrily. "You have a queer way of jesting. I have but one mother, one adorable mother. How could I have two?" and she laughed again.

I saw that there was some mystery I could not unravel at present, and fearing to involve myself in some trouble, refrained from further questioning on the subject. I nevertheless kept a close observance of all that passed, and seized every opportunity to investigate a mystery that began to harass me with its strangeness.

Soon after my conversation with Wauna, I attended an entertainment at which a great number of guests were present. It was a literary festival and, after the intellectual delicacies were disposed of, a banquet followed of more than royal munificence. Toasts were drank, succeeded by music and dancing and all the gayeties of a festive occasion, yet none but the fairest of fair women graced the scene. Is it strange, therefore, that I should have regarded with increasing astonishment and uneasiness a country in all respects alluring to the desires of man—yet found him not there in lordly possession?

Beauty and intellect, wealth and industry, splendor and careful economy, natures lofty and generous, gentle and loving—why has not Man claimed this for himself?

CHAPTER V.

The Preceptress of the National College appointed her daughter Wanna as a guide and instructor to me. I formed a deep and strong attachment for her, which, it pains me to remember, was the cause of her unhappy fate. In stature she was above the medium height, with a form of the fairest earthly loveliness and exquisite grace. Her eyes were so deep a blue, that at first I mistook them for brown. Her hair was the color of a ripe chestnut frosted with gold, and in length and abundance would cover her like a garment. She was vivacious and fond of athletic sports. Her strength amazed me. Those beautiful hands, with their tapering fingers, had a grip like a vise. They had discovered, in this wonderful land, that a body possessing perfectly developed muscles must, by the laws of nature, be symmetrical and graceful. They rode a great deal on small, two-wheeled vehicles, which they propelled themselves. They gave me one on which I accompanied Wauna to all of the places of interest in the Capital city and vicinity.

I must mention that Wauna's voice was exceedingly musical, even in that land of sweet voices, but she did not excel as a singer.

The infant schools interested me more than all the magnificence and grandeur of the college buildings. The quaint courtesy, gentle manners and affectionate demeanor of the little ones toward one another, was a surprise to me. I had visited infant schools of my own and other countries, where I had witnessed the display of human nature, unrestrained by mature discretion and policy. Fights, quarrels, kicks, screams, the unlawful seizure of toys and trinkets, and other misdemeanors, were generally the principal exhibits. But here it was all different. I thought, as I looked at them, that should a philanthropist from the outside world have chanced unknowingly upon the playground of a Mizora infant school, he would have believed himself in a company of little angels.

At first, a kindness so universal impressed me as studied; a species of refined courtesy in which the children were drilled. But time and observation proved to me that it was the natural impulse of the heart, an inherited trait of moral culture. In *my* world, kindness and affection were family possessions, extended occasionally to acquaintances. Beyond this was courtesy only for the great busy bustling mass of humanity called—"the world."

It must not be understood that there was no variety of character in Mizora. Just as marked a difference was to be found there as elsewhere; but it was elevated and ennobled. Its evil tendencies had been eliminated. There were many causes that had made this possible. The first, and probably the most influential, was the extreme cheapness of living. Food and fuel were items of so small consequence, that poverty had become unknown. Added to this, and to me by far the most vital reason, was their system of free education. In contemplating the state of enlightenment to which Mizora had attained, I became an enthusiast upon the subject of education, and resolved, should I ever again reach the upper world, to devote all my energies and ability to convincing the governments of its importance. I believe it is the duty of every government to make its schools and colleges, and everything appertaining to education—FREE. To be always starved for knowledge is a more pitiful craving than to hunger for bread. One dwarfs the body; the other the mind.

The utmost care was bestowed upon the training and education of the children. There was nothing that I met with in that beautiful and happy country I longed more to bring with me to the inhabitants of my world, than their manner of rearing children. The most scrupulous attention was paid to their diet and exercise, both mental and physical. The result was plump limbs, healthy, happy faces and joyous spirits. In all the fifteen years that I spent in Mizora, I never saw a tear of sorrow fall from children's eyes. Admirable sanitary regulations exist in all the cities and villages of the land, which insures them pure air. I may state here that every private-house looks as carefully to the condition of its atmosphere, as we do to the material neatness of ours.

The only intense feeling that I could discover among these people was the love between parent and child. I visited the theater where the tragedy of the play was the destruction of a daughter by shipwreck in view of the distracted mother. The scenery was managed with wonderful realism. The thunder of the surf as it beat upon the shore, the frightful carnival of wind and waves that no human power could still, and the agony of the mother watching the vessel break to pieces upon the rock and her child sink into the boiling water to rise no more, was thrilling beyond my power to describe. I lost control of my feelings. The audience wept and applauded; and when the curtain fell, I could scarcely believe it had only been a play. The love of Mizora women for their children is strong and deep. They consider the care of them a sacred duty, fraught with the noblest results of life. A daughter of scholarly attainments and noble character is a credit to her mother. That selfish mother who looks upon her children as so many afflictions is unknown to Mizora. If a mother should ever feel her children as burdens upon her, she would never give it expression, as any dereliction of duty would be severely rebuked by the whole community, if not punished by banishment. Corporal punishment was unknown.

I received an invitation from a lady prominent in literature and science to make her a visit. I accepted with gratification, as it would afford me the opportunity I coveted to become acquainted with the domestic life of Mizora, and perhaps penetrate its greatest mystery, for I must confess that the singular dearth of anything and everything resembling Man, never ceased to prey upon my curiosity.

The lady was the editor and proprietor of the largest and most widely known scientific and literary magazine in the country. She was the mother of eight children, and possessed one of the largest fortunes and most magnificent residences in the country.

The house stood on an elevation, and was a magnificent structure of grey granite, with polished cornices. The porch floors were of clouded marble. The pillars supporting its roof were round shafts of the same material, with vines of ivy, grape and rose winding about them, carved and colored into perfect representations of the natural shrubs.

The drawing-room, which was vast and imposing in size and appearance, had a floor of pure white marble. The mantels and window-sills were of white onyx, with delicate vinings of pink and green. The floor was strewn with richly colored mats and rugs. Luxurious sofas and chairs comprised the only furniture. Each corner contained a piece of fine statuary. From the centre of the ceiling depended a large gold basin of beautiful design and workmanship, in which played a miniature fountain of perfumed water that filled the air with a delicate fragrance. The walls were divided into panels of polished and unpolished granite. On the unpolished panels hung paintings of scenery. The dull, gray color of the walls brought out in sharp and tasteful relief the few costly and elegant adornments of the room: a placid landscape with mountains dimly outlining the distance. A water scene with a boat idly drifting, occupied by a solitary figure watching the play of variegated lights upon the tranquil waters. Then came a wild and rugged mountain scene with precipices and a foaming torrent. Then a concert of birds amusingly treated.

The onyx marble mantel-piece contained but a single ornament—an orchestra. A coral vase contained a large and perfect tiger lily, made of gold. Each stamen supported a tiny figure carved out of ivory, holding a musical instrument. When they played, each figure appeared instinct with life, like the mythical fairies of my childhood; and the music was so sweet, yet faint, that I readily imagined the charmed ring and tiny dancers keeping time to its rhythm.

The drawing-room presented a vista of arches draped in curtains of a rare texture, though I afterward learned they were spun glass. The one that draped the entrance to the conservatory looked like sea foam with the faint blush of day shining through it. The conservatory was in the shape of a half sphere, and entirely of glass. From its dome, more than a hundred feet above our heads, hung a globe of white fire that gave forth a soft clear light. Terminating, as it did, the long vista of arches with their transparent hangings of cobweb texture, it presented a picture of magnificence and beauty indescribably.

The other apartments displayed the same taste and luxury. The sitting-room contained an instrument resembling a grand piano.

The grounds surrounding this elegant home were adorned with natural and artificial beauties, Grottoes, fountains, lakes, cascades, terraces of flowers, statuary, arbors and foliage in endless variety, that rendered it a miniature paradise. In these grounds, darting in and out among the avenues, playing hide-and-seek behind the statuary, or otherwise amusing themselves, I met eight lovely children, ranging from infancy to young maidenhood. The glowing cheeks and eyes, and supple limbs spoke of perfect health and happiness. When they saw their mother coming, they ran to meet her, the oldest carrying the two-year old baby. The stately woman greeted each with a loving kiss. She showed in loving glance and action how dear they all were to her. For the time being she unbent, and became a child herself in the interest she took in their prattle and mirth. A true mother and happy children.

I discovered that each department of this handsome home was under the care of a professional artist. I remarked to my hostess that I had supposed her home was the expression of her own taste.

"So it is," she replied; "but it requires an equally well educated taste to carry out my designs. The arrangement and ornamentation of my grounds were suggested by me, and planned and executed by my landscape artist."

After supper we repaired to the general sitting-room. The eldest daughter had been deeply absorbed in a book before we came in. She closed and left it upon a table. I watched for an opportunity to carelessly pick it up and examine it. It was a novel I felt sure, for she appeared to resign it reluctantly out of courtesy to her guest. I might, from it, gather some clue to the mystery of the male sex. I took up the book and opened it. It was The Conservation of Force and The Phenomena of Nature. I laid it down with a sigh of discomfiture.

The next evening, my hostess gave a small entertainment, and what was my amazement, not to say offense, to perceive the cook, the chamber-maid, and in fact all the servants in the establishment, enter and join in the conversation and amusement. The cook was asked to sing, for, with the exception of myself—and I tried to conceal it—no one appeared to take umbrage at her presence. She sat down to the piano and sang a pretty ballad in a charming manner. Her voice was cultivated and musical, as are all the voices in Mizora, but it was lacking in the qualities that make a great singer, yet it had a plaintive sweetness that was very attractive.

I was dumbfounded at her presumption. In my country such a thing is unknown as a servant entertaining guests in such a capacity, and especially among people of my rank and position in the world.

I repelled some advances she made me with a hauteur and coldness that it mortified me afterward to remember. Instead of being *my* inferior, I was her's, and she knew it; but neither by look, tone nor action did she betray her consciousness of it. I had to acknowledge that her hands were more delicately modeled than mine, and her bearing had a dignity and elegance that might have been envied by the most aristocratic dame of my own land. Knowing that the Mizora people were peculiar in their social ideas, I essayed to repress my indignation at the time, but later I unburdened myself to Wauna who, with her usual sweetness and gentleness, explained to me that her occupation was a mere matter of choice with her.

"She is one of the most distinguished chemists of this nation. She solved the problem of making bread out of limestone of a much finer quality than had been in use before."

"Don't tell me that you gave me a stone when I asked for bread!" I exclaimed.

"We have not done that," replied Wauna; "but we have given you what you took for bread, but which is manufactured out of limestone and the refuse of the marble quarries."

I looked at her in such inane astonishment that she hastened to add:

"I will take you to one of the large factories some day. They are always in the mountains where the stone is abundant. You can there see loaves by the thousands packed in great glass tanks for shipment to the different markets. And they do not cost the manufacturer above one centime per hundred."

"And what royalty does the discoverer get for this wonder of chemistry?"

"None. Whenever anything of that kind is discovered in our country, it is purchased outright by the government, and then made public for the benefit of all. The competition among manufacturers consists in the care and exactness with which they combine the necessary elements. There is quite a difference in the taste and quality of our bread as it comes from different factories."

"Why doesn't such a talented person quit working in another woman's kitchen and keep herself like a lady?" I inquired, all the prejudice of indolent wealth against labor coming up in my thoughts.

"She has a taste for that kind of work," replied Wauna, "instead of for making dresses, or carving gems, or painting. She often says she could not make a straight line if she tried, yet she can put together with such nicety and chemical skill the elements that form an omelette or a custard, that she has become famous. She teaches all who desire to learn, but none seem to equal her. She was born with a genius for cooking and nothing else. Haven't you seen her with a long glass tube testing the vessels of vegetables and fruit that were cooking?"

"Yes," I answered. "It was from that that I supposed her occupation menial."

"Visitors from other cities," continued Wauna, "nearly always inquire for her first."

Perceiving the mistake that I had made, I ventured an apology for my behavior toward her, and Wauna replied, with a frankness that nearly crushed me:

"We all noticed it, but do not fear a retaliation," she added sweetly. "We know that you are from a civilization that we look back upon as one of barbarism."

I acknowledged that if any superciliousness existed in Mizora while I was there, I must have had it.

The guests departed without refreshments having been served. I explained the custom of entertainment in my country, which elicited expressions of astonishment. It would be insulting to offer refreshments of any kind to a guest between the regular hours for dining, as it would imply a desire on your part to impair their health. Such was the explanation of what in my country would be deemed a gross neglect of duty. Their custom was probably the result of two causes: an enlightened knowledge of the laws of health, and the extreme cheapness of all luxuries of the table which the skill of the chemist had made available to every class of people in the land.

The word "servant" did not exist in the language of Mizora; neither had they an equivalent for it in the sense in which we understand and use the word. I could not tell a servant—for I must use the word to be understood—from a professor in the National College. They were all highly-educated, refined, lady-like and lovely. Their occupations were always matters of choice, for, as there was nothing in them to detract from their social position, they selected the one they knew they had the ability to fill. Hence those positions *we* are accustomed to regard as menial, were there filled by ladies of the highest culture and refinement; consequently the domestic duties of a Mizora household moved to their accomplishment with the ease and regularity of fine machinery.

It was long before I could comprehend the dignity they attached to the humblest vocations. They had one proverb that embraced it all: "Labor is the necessity of life." I studied this peculiar phase of Mizora life, and at last comprehended that in this very law of social equality lay the foundation of their superiority. Their admirable system of adapting the mind to the vocation in which it was most capable of excelling, and endowing that with dignity and respect, and, at the same time, compelling the highest mental culture possible, had produced a nation in the enjoyment of universal refinement, and a higher order of intelligence than any yet known to the outside world.

The standard of an ordinary education was to me astonishingly high. The reason for it was easily understood when informed that the only aristocracy of the country was that of intellect. Scholars, artists, scientists, literateurs, all those excelling in intellectual gifts or attainments, were alone regarded as superiors by the masses.

In all the houses that I had visited I had never seen a portrait hung in a room thrown open to visitors. On inquiry, I was informed that it was a lack of taste to make a portrait conspicuous.

"You meet faces at all times," said my informant, "but you cannot at all times have a variety of scenery before you. How monotonous it would be with a drawing-room full of women, and the walls filled with their painted representatives. We never do it."

"Then where do you keep your family portraits?"

"Ours is in a gallery upstairs."

I requested to be shown this, and was conducted to a very long apartment on the third floor, devoted exclusively to relics and portraits of family ancestry. There were over three thousand portraits of blond women, which my hostess' daughter informed me represented her grandmothers for ages back. Not one word did she say about her grandfathers.

I may mention here that no word existed in their dictionaries that was equivalent to the word "man." I had made myself acquainted with this fact as soon as I had acquired sufficient knowledge of their language. My astonishment at it cannot be described. It was a mystery that became more and more perplexing. Never in the closest intimacy that I could secure could I obtain the slightest clue, the least suggestion relating to the presence of man. My friend's infant, scarcely two years old, prattled of everything but a father.

I cannot explain a certain impressive dignity about the women of Mizora that, in spite of their amiability and winning gentleness, forbade a close questioning into private affairs. My hostess never spoke of her business. It would have been a breach of etiquette to have questioned her about it. I could not bring myself to intrude the question of the marked absence of men, when not the slightest allusion was ever made to them by any citizen.

So time passed on, confirming my high opinion of them, and yet I knew and felt and believed that some strange and incomprehensible mystery surrounded them, and when I had abandoned all hope of a solution to it, it solved itself in the most unexpected and yet natural manner, and I was more astonished at the solution than I was at the mystery.

CHAPTER VI.

Their domestic life was so harmonious and perfect that it was a perpetual pleasure to contemplate.

Human nature finds its sweetest pleasure, its happiest content, within its own home circle; and in Mizora I found no exception to the rule. The arrangement and adornment of every house in Mizora were evidently for the comfort and happiness of its inmates. To purchase anything for merely outside show, or to excite the envy or jealousy of a neighbor, was never thought of by an inhabitant of Mizora.

The houses that were built to rent excited my admiration quite as much as did the private residences. They all seemed to have been designed with two special objects in view—beauty and comfort. Houses built to rent in large cities were always in the form of a hollow square, inclosing a commodious and handsomely decorated park. The back was adorned with an upper and lower piazza opening upon the park. The suites of rooms were so arranged as to exclusively separate their occupants from all others. The park was undivided. The center was occupied by a fountain large enough to shoot its spray as high as the uppermost piazza. The park was furnished with rustic seats and shade trees, frequently of immense size, branched above its smooth walks and promenades, where baby wagons, velocipedes and hobby horses on wheels could have uninterrupted sport.

Suburban residences, designed for rent, were on a similar but more amplified plan. The houses were detached, but the grounds were in common. Many private residences were also constructed on the same plan. Five or six acres would be purchased by a dozen families who were not rich enough to own large places separately. A separate residence would be built for each family, but the ground would be laid off and ornamented like a private park. Each of the dozen families would thus have a beautiful view and the privilege of the whole ground. In this way, cascades, fountains, rustic arbors, rockeries, aquariums, tiny lakes, and every variety of landscape ornamenting, could be supplied at a comparatively small cost to each family.

Should any one wish to sell, they disposed of their house and one-twelfth of the undivided ground, and a certain per cent. of the value of its ornaments. The established custom was never to remove or alter property thus purchased without the consent of the other shareholders. Where a people had been educated to regard justice and conscience as their law, such an arrangement could be beneficial to an entire city.

Financial ability does not belong to every one, and this plan of uniting small capitals gave opportunity to the less wealthy classes to enjoy all the luxuries that belong to the rich. In fact some of the handsomest parks I saw in Mizora were owned and kept up in this manner. Sometimes as many as twenty families united in the purchase of an estate, and constructed artificial lakes large enough to sail upon. Artificial cascades and fountains of wonderful size and beauty were common ornaments in all the private and public parks of the city. I noticed in all the cities that I visited the beauty and charm of the public parks, which were found in all sections.

The walks were smoothly paved and shaded by trees of enormous size. They were always frequented by children, who could romp and play in these sylvan retreats of beauty in perfect security.

The high state of culture arrived at by the Mizora people rendered a luxurious style of living a necessity to all. Many things that I had been brought up to regard as the exclusive privileges of the rich, were here the common pleasure of every one. There was no distinction of classes; no genteel-poverty people, who denied themselves necessities that they might appear to have luxuries. There was not a home in Mizora that I entered—and I had access to many—that did not give the impression of wealth in all its appointments.

I asked the Preceptress to explain to me how I might carry back to the people of my country this social happiness, this equality of physical comfort and luxury; and she answered me with emphasis:

"Educate them. Convince the rich that by educating the poor, they are providing for their own safety. They will have fewer prisons to build, fewer courts to sustain. Educated Labor will work out its own salvation against Capital. Let the children of toil start in life with exactly the same educational advantages that are enjoyed by the rich. Give them the same physical and moral training, and let the rich pay for it by taxes."

I shook my head "They will never submit to it," was my reluctant admission.

"Appeal to their selfishness," urged the Preceptress "Get them to open their college doors and ask all to come and be taught without money and without price. The power of capital is great, but stinted and ignorant toil will rise against its oppression, and innocence and guilt will alike suffer from its fury. Have you never known such an occurrence?"

"Not in my day or country," I answered "But the city in which I was educated has such a history. Its gutters flowed with human blood, the blood of its nobles."

She inclined her head significantly. "It will be repeated," she said sadly, "unless you educate them. Give their bright and active minds the power of knowledge. They will use it wisely, for their own and their country's welfare."

I doubted my ability to do this, to contend against rooted and inherited prejudice, but I resolved to try. I did not need to be told that the rich and powerful had a monopoly of intellect: Nature was not partial to them, for the children of the poor, I well knew, were often handsomer and more intellectual than the offspring of wealth and aristocratic birth.

I have before spoken of the positions occupied by those who performed what I had been bred to regard as menial work. At first, the mere fact of the person who presided over the kitchen being presented to me as an equal, was outraging to all my hereditary dignity and pride of birth. No one could be more pronounced in a consciousness of inherited nobility than I. I had been taught from infancy to regard myself as a superior being, merely because the accident of birth had made me so, and the arrogance with which I had treated some of my less favored schoolmates reverted to me with mortifying regret, when, having asked Wauna to point out to me the nobly born, she looked at me with her sweet expression of candor and innocence and said:

"We have no nobility of birth. As I once before told you, intellect is our only standard of excellence. It alone occupies an exalted place and receives the homage of our people."

In a subsequent conversation with her mother, the Preceptress, she said:

"In remote ages, great honor and deference was paid to all who were born of rulers, and the designation 'noble blood,' was applied to them. At one time in the history of our country they could commit any outrage upon society or morals without fear of punishment, simply because they belonged to the aristocracy. Even a heinous murder would be unnoticed if perpetrated by one of them. Nature alone did not favor them Imbecile and immoral minds fell to the lot of the aristocrat as often as to the lowly born. Nature's laws are inflexible and swerve not for any human wish. They outraged them by the admixture of kindred blood, and degeneracy was often the result. A people should always have for their chief ruler the highest and noblest intellect among them, but in those dark ages they were too often compelled to submit to the lowest, simply because it had been *born* to the position. But," she added, with a sweet smile, "*that* time lies many centuries behind us, and I sometimes think we had better forget it entirely."

My first meeting with the domestics of my friend's house impressed me with their high mental culture, refinement and elegance. Certainly no "grande dame" of my own country but would have been proud of their beauty and graceful dignity.

Prejudice, however deeply ingrained, could not resist the custom of a whole country, and especially such a one as Mizora, so I soon found myself on a familiar footing with my friend's "artist"—for the name by which they were designated as a class had very nearly the same meaning.

Cooking was an art, and one which the people of Mizora had cultivated to the highest excellence. It is not strange, when their enlightenment is understood, that they should attach as much honor to it as the people of my country do to sculpture, painting and literature. The Preceptress told me that such would be the case with my people when education became universal and the poor could start in life with the same intellectual culture as the rich. The chemistry of food and its importance in preserving a youthful vigor and preventing disease, would then be understood and appreciated by all classes, and would receive the deference it deserved.

"You will never realize," said the Preceptress earnestly, "the incalculable benefit that will accrue to your people from educating your poor. Urge that Government to try it for just twenty years, long enough for a generation to be born and mature. The bright and eager intellects of poverty will turn to Chemistry to solve the problems of cheap Light, cheap Fuel and cheap Food. When you can clothe yourselves from the fibre of the trees, and warm and light your dwellings from the water of your rivers, and eat of the stones of the earth, Poverty and Disease will be as unknown to your people as it is to mine."

"If I should preach that to them, they would call me a maniac."

"None but the ignorant will do so. From your description of the great thinkers of your country, I am inclined to believe there are minds among you advanced enough to believe in it."

I remembered how steamboats and railroads and telegraphy had been opposed and ridiculed until proven practicable, and I took courage and resolved to follow the advice of my wise counselor.

I had long felt a curiosity to behold the inner workings of a domestic's life, and one day ventured to ask my friend's permission to enter her kitchen. Surprise was manifested at such a request, when I began to apologize and explain. But my hostess smiled and said:

"My kitchen is at all times as free to my guests as my drawing room."

Every kitchen in Mizora is on the same plan and conducted the same way. To describe one, therefore, is to describe all. I undertook to explain that in my country, good breeding forbade a guest entering the host's kitchen, and frequently its appearance, and that of the cook's, would not conduce to gastric enjoyment of the edibles prepared in it.

My first visit happened to be on scrubbing day, and I was greatly amused to see a little machine, with brushes and sponges attached, going over the floor at a swift rate, scouring and sponging dry as it went. Two vessels, one containing soap suds and the other clear water, were connected by small feed pipes with the brushes. As soon as the drying sponge became saturated, it was lifted by an ingenious yet simple contrivance into a vessel and pressed dry, and was again dropped to the floor.

I inquired how it was turned to reverse its progress so as to clean the whole floor, and was told to watch when it struck the wall. I did so, and saw that the jar not only reversed the machine, but caused it to spring to the right about two feet, which was its width, and again begin work on a new line, to be again reversed in the same manner when it struck the opposite wall. Carpeted floors were swept by a similar contrivance.

No wonder the "artists" of the kitchen had such a dainty appearance. They dipped their pretty hands in perfumed water and dried them on the finest and whitest damask, while machinery did the coarse work.

Mizora, I discovered, was a land of brain workers. In every vocation of life machinery was called upon to perform the arduous physical labor. The whole domestic department was a marvel of ingenious mechanical contrivances. Dishwashing, scouring and cleaning of every description were done by machinery.

The Preceptress told me that it was the result of enlightenment, and it would become the custom in my country to make machinery perform the laborious work when they learned the value of universal and advanced knowledge.

I observed that the most exact care was given to the preparation of food. Every cook was required to be a chemist of the highest excellence; another thing that struck me as radically different from the custom in vogue in my country.

Everything was cooked by hot air and under cover, so that no odor was perceptible in the room. Ventilating pipes conveyed the steam from cooking food out of doors. Vegetables and fruits appeared to acquire a richer flavor when thus cooked. The seasoning was done by exact weight and measure, and there was no stirring or tasting. A glass tube, on the principle of a thermometer, determined when each article was done. The perfection which they had attained as culinary chemists was a source of much gratification to me, both in the taste of food so delicious and palatable, and in its wholesome effect on my constitution. As to its deliciousness, a meal prepared by a Mizora cook could rival the fabled feasts of the gods. Its beneficial effects upon me were manifested in a healthier tone of body and an an increase of animal spirits, a pleasurable feeling of content and amiability.

The Preceptress told me that the first step toward the eradication of disease was in the scientific preparation of food, and the establishment of schools where cooking was taught as an art to all who applied, and without charge. Placed upon a scientific basis it became respectable.

"To eliminate from our food the deleterious earthy matter is our constant aim. To that alone do we owe immunity from old age far in advance of that period of life when your people become decrepit and senile. The human body is like a lamp-wick, which filters the oil while it furnishes light. In time the wick becomes clogged and useless and is thrown away. If the oil could be made perfectly pure, the wick would not fill up."

She gave this homely explanation with a smile and the air of a grown person trying to convey to the immature mind of a child an explanation of some of Nature's phenomena.

I reflected upon their social condition and arrived at the conviction that there is no occupation in life but what has its usefulness and necessity, and, when united to culture and refinement, its dignity. A tree has a million leaves, yet each individual leaf, insignificant as it may appear, has its special share of work to perform in helping the tree to live and perfect its fruit. So should every citizen of a government contribute to its vitality and receive a share of its benefits.

"Will the time ever come," I asked myself, "when my own country will see this and rise to a social, if not intellectual equality." And the admonition of the Preceptress would recur to my mind:

"Educate them. Educate them, and enlightenment will solve for them every problem in Sociology."

My observations in Mizora led me to believe that while Nature will permit and encourage the outgrowth of equality in refinement, she gives birth to a more decided prominence in the leadership of intellect.

The lady who conducted me through the culinary department, and pointed out the machinery and explained its use and convenience, had the same grace and dignity of manner as the hostess displayed when exhibiting to me the rare plants in her conservatory.

The laundry was a separate business. No one unconnected with it as a profession had anything to do with its duties. I visited several of the large city laundries and was informed that all were conducted alike. Steam was employed in the cleaning process, and the drying was done by hot air impregnated with ozone. This removed from white fabrics every vestige of discoloration or stain. I saw twelve dozen fine damask table-cloths cleaned, dried and ironed in thirty minutes. All done by machinery. They emerged from the rollers that ironed them looking like new pieces of goods, so pure was their color, and so glossy their finish.

I inquired the price for doing them up, and was told a cent a piece. Twelve cents per dozen was the established price for doing up clothes. Table-cloths and similar articles were ironed between rollers constructed to admit their full width. Other articles of more complicated make, were ironed by machines constructed to suit them. Some articles were dressed by having hot air forced rapidly through them. Lace curtains, shawls, veils, spreads, tidies and all similar articles, were by this process made to look like new, and at a cost that I thought ought certainly to reduce the establishment to beggary or insolvency. But here chemistry again was the magician that had made such cheap labor profitable. And such advanced knowledge of chemistry was the result of universal education.

Ladies sent their finest laces to be renewed without fear of having them reduced to shreds. In doing up the frailest laces, nothing but hot air impregnated with ozone was employed. These were consecutively forced through the fabric after it was carefully stretched. Nothing was ever lost or torn, so methodical was the management of the work.

I asked why cooking was not established as the laundry was, as a distinct public business, and was told that it had been tried a number of times, but had always been found impracticable. One kind of work in a laundry would suit everyone, but one course of cooking could not. Tastes and appetites differed greatly. What was palatable to one would be disliked by another, and to prepare food for a large number of customers, without knowing or being able to know exactly what the demand would be, had always resulted in large waste, and as the people of Mizora were the most rigid and exacting economists, it was not to be wondered at that they had selected the most economical plan. Every private cook could determine accurately the amount of food required for the household she prepared it for, and knowing their tastes she could cater to all without waste.

"We, as yet," said my distinguished instructor, "derive all our fruit and vegetables from the soil. We have orchards and vineyards and gardens which we carefully tend, and which our knowledge of chemistry enables us to keep in health and productiveness. But there is always more or less earthy matter in all food derived from cultivating the soil, and the laboratories are now striving to produce artificial fruit and vegetables that will satisfy the palate and be free from deleterious matter."

CHAPTER VII.

One of the most curious and pleasing sights in Mizora was the flower gardens and conservatories. Roses of all sizes and colors and shades of color were there. Some two feet across were placed by the side of others not exceeding the fourth of an inch in order to display the disparity in size.

To enter into a minute description of all the discoveries made by the Mizora people in fruit and floriculture, would be too tedious; suffice to say they had laid their hands upon the beautiful and compelled nature to reveal to them the secret of its formation. The number of petals, their color, shape and size, were produced as desired. The only thing they could neither create nor destroy was its perfume. I questioned the Preceptress as to the possibility of its ever being discovered? She replied:

"It is the one secret of the rose that Nature refuses to reveal. I do not believe we shall ever possess the power to increase or diminish the odor of a flower. I believe that Nature will always reserve to herself the secret of its creation. The success that we enjoy in the wonderful cultivation of our fruits and flowers was one of our earliest scientific conquests."

I learned that their orchards never failed to yield a bounteous harvest. They had many fruits that were new to me, and some that were new and greatly improved species of kinds that I had already seen and eaten in my own or other countries. Nothing that they cultivated was ever without its own peculiar beauty as well as usefulness. Their orchards, when the fruit was ripe, presented a picture of unique charm. Their trees were always trained into graceful shapes, and when the ripe fruit gleamed through the dark green foliage, every tree looked like a huge bouquet. A cherry tree that I much admired, and the fruit of which I found surpassingly delicious, I must allow myself to describe. The cherries were not surprisingly large, but were of the colors and transparency of honey. They were seedless, the tree having to be propagated from slips. When the fruit was ripe the tree looked like a huge ball of pale amber gems hiding in the shadows of dark pointed leaves.

Their grape arbors were delightful pictures in their season of maturity. Some vines had clusters of fruit three feet long; but these I was told were only to show what they *could* do in grape culture. The usual and marketable size of a bunch was from one to two pounds weight. The fruit was always perfect that was offered for sale.

Science had provided the fruit growers of Mizora with permanent protections from all kinds of blight or decay.

When I considered the wholesomeness of all kinds of food prepared for the inhabitants of this favored land. I began to think they might owe a goodly portion of their exceptional health to it, and a large share of their national amiability to their physical comfort. I made some such observation to the Preceptress, and she admitted its correctness.

"The first step that my people made toward the eradication of disease was in the preparation of healthy food; not for the rich, who could obtain it themselves, but for the whole nation."

I asked for further information and she added:

"Science discovered that mysterious and complicated diseases often had their origin in adulterated food. People suffered and died, ignorant of what produced their disease. The law, in the first place, rigidly enforced the marketing of clean and perfect fruit, and a wholesome quality of all other provisions. This was at first difficult to do, as in those ancient days, (I refer to a very remote period of our history) in order to make usurious profit, dealers adulterated all kinds of food; often with poisonous substances. When every state took charge of its markets and provided free schools for cooking, progress took a rapid advance. Do you wonder at it? Reflect then. How could I force my mind into complete absorption of some new combination of chemicals, while the gastric juice in my stomach was battling with sour or adulterated food? Nature would compel me to pay some attention to the discomfort of my digestive organs, and it might happen at a time when I was on the verge of a revelation in science, which might be lost. You may think it an insignificant matter to speak of in connection with the grand enlightenment that we possess; but Nature herself is a mass of little things. Our bodies, strong and supple as they are, are nothing but a union of tiny cells. It is by the investigation of little things that we have reached the great ones."

I felt a keen desire to know more about their progress toward universal health, feeling assured that the history of the extirpation of disease must be curious and instructive. I had been previously made acquainted with the fact that disease was really unknown to them, save in its historical existence. To cull this isolated history from their vast libraries of past events, would require a great deal of patient and laborious research, and the necessary reading of a great deal of matter that I could not be interested in, and that could not beside be of any real value to me, so I requested the Preceptress to give me an epitomized history of it in her own language, merely relating such facts as might be useful to me, and that I could comprehend, for I may as well bring forward the fact that, in comparison to theirs, my mind was as a savages would be to our civilization.

Their brain was of a finer intellectual fiber. It possessed a wider, grander, more majestic receptivity. They absorbed ideas that passed over me like a cloud. Their imaginations were etherealized. They reached into what appeared to be materialless space, and brought from it substances I had never heard of before, and by processes I could not comprehend. They divided matter into new elements and utilized them. They disintegrated matter, added to it new properties and produced a different material. I saw the effects and uses of their chemistry, but that was all.

There are minds belonging to my own age, as there have been to all ages, that are intellectually in advance of it. They live in a mental and prophetic world of their own, and leave behind them discoveries, inventions and teachings that benefit and ennoble the generations to come. Could such a mind have chanced upon Mizora, as I chanced upon it, it might have consorted with its intellect, and brought from the companionship ideas that I could not receive, and sciences that I can find no words in my language to represent. The impression that my own country might make upon a savage, may describe my relation to Mizora. What could an uncivilized mind say of our railroads, or magnificent cathedrals, our palaces, our splendor, our wealth, our works of art. They would be as difficult of representation as were the lofty aims, the unselfishness in living, the perfect love, honor and intellectual grandeur, and the universal comfort and luxury found in Mizora, were to me. To them the cultivation of the mind was an imperative duty, that neither age nor condition retarded. To do good, to be approved by their own conscience, was their constant pleasure.

CHAPTER VIII.

It was during my visit at my friend's house that I first witnessed the peculiar manner in which the markets in Mizora are conducted. Everything, as usual, was fastidiously neat and clean. The fruit and vegetables were fresh and perfect. I examined quantities of them to satisfy myself, and not a blemish or imperfection could be found on any. None but buyers were attending market. Baskets of fruit, bunches of vegetables and, in fact, everything exhibited for sale, had the quality and the price labeled upon it. Small wicker baskets were near to receive the change. When a buyer had selected what suited her, she dropped the label and the change in the basket. I saw one basket filled with gold and silver coin, yet not one would be missing when the owner came to count up the sales. Sometimes a purchaser was obliged to change a large piece of money, but it was always done accurately.

There was one singular trait these people possessed that, in conjunction with their other characteristics, may seem unnatural: they would give and exact the last centime (a quarter of a cent) in a trade. I noticed this peculiarity so frequently that I inquired the reason for it, and when I had studied it over I decided that, like all the other rules that these admirable people had established, it was wise. Said my friend:

"We set a just value on everything we prepare for sale. Anything above or below that, would be unjust to buyer or seller."

The varieties of apples, pears, peaches and other fruits had their names attached, with the quality, sweet, sour, or slightly acid. In no instance was it found to be incorrectly stated. I came to one stall that contained nothing but glass jars of butter and cream. The butter was a rich buff color, like very fine qualities I had seen in my own country. The cream, an article I am fond of drinking, looked so tempting I longed to purchase a glass for that purpose. The lady whom I accompanied (my hostess' cook) informed me that it was artificially prepared. The butter and cheese were chemical productions. Different laboratories produced articles of varying flavor, according to the chemist's skill. Although their construction was no secret, yet some laboratories enjoyed special reputation for their butter and cheese owing to the accuracy with which their elements were combined.

She gave me quite a history about artificial food, also how they kept fruits and vegetables in their natural state for years without decaying or losing their flavor, so that when eaten they were nearly as fine as when freshly gathered. After hearing that the cream was manufactured, I resolved to taste it. Dropping my coin into the basket, I took up a glass and drank it. A look of disgust crossed the countenance of my companion.

"Do you not drink this?" I asked in surprise, as I set down the empty vessel. "It is truly delicious."

"At regular meal times we all use it, and sometimes drink it in preference to other beverages—but never in public. You will never see a citizen of Mizora eating in public.

Look all over this market and you will not discover one person, either adult or child, eating or drinking, unless it be water."

I could not; and I felt keenly mortified at my mistake. Yet in my own country and others that, according to our standard, are highly civilized, a beverage is made from the juice of the corn that is not only drank in public places, but its effects, which are always unbecoming, are exhibited also, and frequently without reproof. However, I said nothing to my companion about this beverage. It bears no comparison in color or taste to that made in Mizora. I could not have distinguished the latter from the finest dairy cream.

The next place of interest that I visited were their mercantile bazars or stores. Here I found things looking quite familiar. The goods were piled upon shelves behind counters, and numerous clerks were in attendance. It was the regular day for shopping among the Mizora ladies, and the merchants had made a display of their prettiest and richest goods. I noticed the ladies were as elegantly dressed as if for a reception, and learned that it was the custom. They would meet a great many friends and acquaintances, and dressed to honor the occasion.

It was my first shopping experience in Mizora, and I quite mortified myself by removing my glove and rubbing and examining closely the goods I thought of purchasing. I entirely ignored the sweet voice of the clerk that was gently informing me that it was "pure linen" or "pure wool," so habituated had I become in my own country to being my own judge of the quality of the goods I was purchasing, regardless always of the seller's recommendation of it. I found it difficult, especially in such circumstances, to always remember their strict adherence to honesty and fair dealing. I felt rebuked when I looked around and saw the actions of the other ladies in buying.

In manufactured goods, as in all other things, not the slightest cheatery is to be found. Woolen and cotton mixtures were never sold for pure wool. Nobody seemed to have heard of the art of glossing muslin cuffs and collars and selling them for pure linen.

Fearing that I had wounded the feelings of the lady in attendance upon me, I hastened to apologize by explaining the peculiar methods of trade that were practiced in my own country. They were immediately pronounced barbarous.

I noticed that ladies in shopping examined colors and effects of trimmings or combinations, but never examined the quality. Whatever the attendant said about *that* was received as a fact.

The reason for the absence of attendants in the markets and the presence of them in mercantile houses was apparent at once. The market articles were brought fresh every day, while goods were stored.

Their business houses and their manner of shopping were unlike anything I had ever met with before. The houses were all built in a hollow square, enclosing a garden with a fountain in the center. These were invariably roofed over with glass, as was the entire building. In winter the garden was as warm as the interior of the store. It was adorned with flowers and shrubs. I often saw ladies and children promenading in these pretty inclosures, or sitting on their rustic sofas conversing, while their friends were shopping in the store. The arrangement gave perfect light and comfort to both clerks and customers, and the display of rich and handsome fabrics was enhanced by the bit of scenery beyond. In summer the water for the fountain was artificially cooled.

Every clerk was provided with a chair suspended by pulleys from strong iron rods fastened above. They could be raised or lowered at will; and when not occupied, could be drawn up out of the way. After the goods were purchased, they were placed in a machine that wrapped and tied them ready for delivery.

A dining-room was always a part of every store. I desired to be shown this, and found it as tasteful and elegant in its appointments as a private one would be. Silver and china and fine damask made it inviting to the eye, and I had no doubt the cooking corresponded as well with the taste.

The streets of Mizora were all paved, even the roads through the villages were furnished an artificial cover, durable, smooth and elastic. For this purpose a variety of materials were used. Some had artificial stone, in the manufacture of which Mizora could surpass nature's production. Artificial wood they also made and used for pavements, as well as cement made of fine sand. The latter was the least durable, but possessed considerable elasticity and made a very fine driving park. They were experimenting when I came away on sanded glass for road beds. The difficulty was to overcome its susceptibility to attrition. After business hours every street was swept by a machine. The streets and sidewalks, in dry weather, were as free from soil as the floor of a private-house would be.

Animals and domestic fowls had long been extinct in Mizora. This was one cause of the weird silence that so impressed me on my first view of their capital city. Invention had superceded the usefulness of animals in all departments: in the field and the chemistry of food. Artificial power was utilized for all vehicles.

The vehicle most popular with the Mizora ladies for shopping and culling purposes, was a very low carriage, sometimes with two seats, sometimes with one. They were upholstered with the richest fabrics, were exceedingly light and graceful in shape, and not above three feet from the ground. They were strong and durable, though frequently not exceeding fifty pounds in weight. The wheel was the curious and ingenious part of the structure, for in its peculiar construction lay the delight of its motion. The spokes were flat bands of steel, curved outward to the tire. The carriage had no spring other than these spokes, yet it moved like a boat gliding down stream with the current. I was fortunate enough to preserve a drawing of this wheel, which I hope some day to introduce in my own land. The carriages were propelled by compressed air or electricity; and sometimes with a mechanism that was simply pressed with the foot. I liked the compressed air best. It was most easily managed by me. The Mizora ladies preferred electricity, of which I was always afraid. They were experimenting with a new propelling power during my stay that was to be acted upon by light, but it had not come into general use, although I saw some vehicles that were propelled by it. They moved with incredible speed, so rapid indeed, that the upper part of the carriage had to be constructed of glass, and securely closed while in motion, to protect the occupant. It was destined, I heard some of their scientists say, to become universal, as it was the most economical power yet discovered. They patiently tried to explain it to me, but my faculties were not receptive to such advanced philosophy, and I had to abandon the hope of ever introducing it into my own country.

There was another article manufactured in Mizora that excited my wonder and admiration. It was elastic glass. I have frequently mentioned the unique uses that they made of it, and I must now explain why. They had discovered a process to render it as pliable as rubber. It was more useful than rubber could be, for it was almost indestructible. It had superceded iron in many ways. All cooking utensils were made of it. It entered largely into the construction and decoration of houses. All cisterns and cellars had an inner lining of it. All underground pipes were made of it, and many things that are the necessities and luxuries of life.

They spun it into threads as fine and delicate as a spider's gossamer, and wove it into a network of clear or variegated colors that dazzled the eye to behold. Innumerable were the lovely fabrics made of it. The frailest lace, in the most intricate and aerial patterns, that had the advantage of never soiling, never tearing, and never wearing out. Curtains for drawing-room arches were frequently made of it. Some of them looked like woven dew drops.

One set of curtains that I greatly admired, and was a long time ignorant of what they were made of, were so unique, I must do myself the pleasure to describe them. They hung across the arch that led to the glass conservatory attached to my friend's handsome dwelling. Three very thin sheets of glass were woven separately and then joined at the edges so ingeniously as to defy detection. The inside curtain was one solid color: crimson. Over this was a curtain of snow flakes, delicate as those aerial nothings of the sky, and more durable than any fabric known. Hung across the arched entrance to a conservatory, with a great globe of white fire shining through it, it was lovely as the blush of Aphrodite when she rose from the sea, veiled in its fleecy foam.

They also possessed the art of making glass highly refractive. Their table-ware surpassed in beauty all that I had ever previously seen. I saw tea cups as frail looking as soap bubbles, possessing the delicate iridescence of opals. Many other exquisite designs were the product of its flexibility and transparency. The first article that attracted my attention was the dress of an actress on the stage. It was lace, made of gossamer threads of amber in the design of lilies and leaves, and was worn over black velvet.

The wonderful water scene that I beheld at the theatre was produced by waves made of glass and edged with foam, a milky glass spun into tiny bubbles. They were agitated by machinery that caused them to roll with a terribly natural look. The blinding flashes of lightning had been the display of genuine electricity.

Nothing in the way of artistic effect could call forth admiration or favorable comment unless it was so exact an imitation of nature as to not be distinguished from the real without the closest scrutiny. In private life no one assumed a part. All the acting I ever saw in Mizora was done upon the stage.

I could not appreciate their mental pleasures, any more than a savage could delight in a nocturne of Chopin. Yet one was the intellectual ecstasy of a sublime intelligence, and the other the harmonious rapture of a divinely melodious soul. I must here mention that the processes of chemical experiment in Mizora differed materially from those I had known. I had once seen and tasted a preparation called artificial cream that had been prepared by a friend of my fathers, an eminent English chemist. It was simply a combination of the known properties of cream united in the presence of gentle heat. But in Mizora they took certain chemicals and converted them into milk, and cream, and cheese, and butter, and every variety of meat, in a vessel that admitted neither air nor light. They claimed that the elements of air and light exercised a material influence upon the chemical production of foods, that they could not be made successfully by artificial processes when exposed to those two agents. Their earliest efforts had been unsuccessful of exact imitation, and a perfect result had only been obtained by closely counterfeiting the processes of nature.

The cream prepared artificially that I had tasted in London, was the same color and consistency as natural cream, but it lacked its relish. The cream manufactured in Mizora was a perfect imitation of the finest dairy product.

It was the same with meats; they combined the elements, and the article produced possessed no detrimental flavor. It was a more economical way of obtaining meat than by fattening animals.

They were equally fortunate in the manufacture of clothing. Every mountain was a cultivated forest, from which they obtained every variety of fabric; silks, satins, velvets, laces, woolen goods, and the richest articles of beauty and luxury, in which to array themselves, were put upon the market at a trifling cost, compared to what they were manufactured at in my own country. Pallid and haggard women and children, working incessantly for a pittance that barely sustained existence, was the ultimatum that the search after the cause of cheap prices arrived at in my world, but here it traveled from one bevy of beautiful workwoman to another until it ended at the Laboratory where Science sat throned, the grand, majestic, humane Queen of this thrice happy land.

CHAPTER IX.

Whenever I inquired:

"From whence comes the heat that is so evenly distributed throughout the dwellings and public buildings of Mizora?" they invariably pointed to the river. I asked in astonishment:

"From water comes fire?"

And they answered: "Yes."

I had long before this time discovered that Mizora was a nation of very wonderful people, individually and collectively; and as every revelation of their genius occurred, I would feel as though I could not be surprised at any marvelous thing that they should claim to do, but I was really not prepared to believe that they could set the river on fire. Yet I found that such was, scientifically, the fact. It was one of their most curious and, at the same time, useful appliances of a philosophical discovery.

They separated water into its two gases, and then, with their ingenious chemical skill, converted it into an economical fuel.

Their coal mines had long been exhausted, as had many other of nature's resources for producing artificial heat. The dense population made it impracticable to cultivate forests for fuel. Its rapid increase demanded of Science the discovery of a fuel that could be consumed without loss to them, both in the matter consumed and in the expense of procuring it. Nothing seemed to answer their purpose so admirably as water. Water, when decomposed, becomes gas. Convert the gas into heat and it becomes water again. A very great heat produces only a small quantity of water: hence the extreme utility of water as a heat producing agent.

The heating factories were all detached buildings, and generally, if at all practicable, situated near a river, or other body of water. Every precaution against accident was stringently observed.

There were several processes for decomposing the water explained to me, but the one preferred, and almost universally used by the people of Mizora, was electricity. The gases formed at the opposite poles of the electrical current, were received in large glass reservoirs, especially constructed for them.

In preparing the heat that gave such a delightful temperature to the dwellings and public buildings of their vast cities, glass was always the material used in the construction of vessels and pipes. Glass pipes conveyed the separate gases of hydrogen and oxygen into an apartment especially prepared for the purpose, and united them upon ignited carbon. The heat produced was intense beyond description, and in the hands of less experienced and capable chemists, would have proved destructful to life and property. The hardest rock would melt in its embrace; yet, in the hands of these wonderful students of Nature, it was under perfect control and had been converted into one of the most healthful and agreeable agents of comfort and usefulness known.

It was regulated with the same ease and convenience with which we increase or diminish the flames of a gas jet. It was conducted, by means of glass pipes, to every dwelling in the city. One factory supplied sufficient heat for over half a million inhabitants.

I thought I was not so far behind Mizora in a knowledge of heating with hot air; yet, when I saw the practical application of their method, I could see no resemblance to that in use in my own world. In winter, every house in Mizora had an atmosphere throughout as balmy as the breath of the young summer. Country-houses and farm dwellings were all supplied with the same kind of heat.

In point of economy it could not be surpassed. A city residence, containing twenty rooms of liberal size and an immense conservatory, was heated entire, at a cost of four hundred centimes a year. One dollar per annum for fuel.

There was neither smoke, nor soot, nor dust. Instead of entering a room through a register, as I had always seen heated air supplied, it came through numerous small apertures in the walls of a room quite close to the floor, thus rendering its supply imperceptible, and making a draft of cold air impossible.

The extreme cheapness of artificial heat made a conservatory a necessary luxury of every dwelling. The same pipes that supplied the dwelling rooms with warmth, supplied the hot-house also, but it was conveyed to the plants by a very different process.

They used electricity in their hot-houses to perfect their fruit, but in what way I could not comprehend; neither could I understand their method of supplying plants and fruits with carbonic acid gas. They manufactured it and turned it into their hot-houses during sleeping hours. No one was permitted to enter until the carbon had been absorbed. They had an instrument resembling a thermometer which gave the exact condition of the atmosphere. They were used in every house, as well as in the conservatories. The people of Mizora were constantly experimenting with those two chemical agents, electricity and carbonic acid gas, in their conservatories. They confidently believed that with their service, they could yet produce fruit from their hot-houses, that would equal in all respects the season grown article.

They produced very fine hot-house fruit. It was more luscious than any artificially ripened fruit that I had ever tasted in my own country, yet it by no means compared with their season grown fruit. Their preserved fruit I thought much more natural in flavor than their hot-house fruit.

Many of their private greenhouses were on a grand scale and contained fruit as well as flowers. A family that could not have a hot-house for fresh vegetables, with a few fruit trees in it, would be poor indeed. Where a number of families had united in purchasing extensive grounds, very fine conservatories were erected, their expense being divided among the property holders, and their luxuries enjoyed in common.

So methodical were all the business plans of the Mizora people, and so strictly just were they in the observance of all business and social duties that no ill-feeling or jealousy could arise from a combination of capital in private luxuries. Such combinations were formed and carried out upon strictly business principles.

If the admirable economy with which every species of work was carried on in Mizora could be thoroughly comprehended, the universality of luxuries need not be wondered at. They were drilled in economy from a very early period. It was taught them as a virtue.

Machinery, with them, had become the slave of invention. I lived long enough in Mizora to comprehend that the absence of pauperism, genteel and otherwise, was largely due to the ingenious application of machinery to all kinds of physical labor. When the cost of producing luxuries decreases, the value of the luxuries produced must decrease with it. The result is they are within reach of the narrowest incomes. A life surrounded by refinement must absorb some of it.

I had a conversation with the Preceptress upon this subject, and she said:

"Some natures are so undecided in character that they become only what their surroundings make them. Others only partially absorb tastes and sentiments that form the influence about them. They maintain a decided individuality; yet they are most always noticeably marked with the general character of their surroundings. It is very, very seldom that a nature is fixed from infancy in one channel."

I told her that I knew of a people whose minds from infancy to mature age, never left the grooves they were born in. They belonged to every nationality, and had palaces built for them, and attendants with cultivated intelligences employed to wait upon them.

"Are their minds of such vast importance to their nation? You have never before alluded to intellect so elevated as to command such royal homage." My friend spoke with awakened interest.

"They are of no importance at all," I answered, humiliated at having alluded to them. "Some of them have not sufficient intelligence to even feed themselves."

"And what are they?" she inquired anxiously.

"They are idiots; human vegetables."

"And you build palaces for them, and hire servants to feed and tend them, while the bright, ambitious children of the poor among you, struggle and suffer for mental advancement. How deplorably short-sighted are the wise ones of your world. Truly it were better in your country to be born an idiot than a poor genius." She sighed and looked grave.

"What should we do with them?" I inquired.

"What do you do with the useless weeds in your garden," she asked significantly. "Do you carefully tend them, while drouth and frost and lack of nourishment cause your choice plants to wither and die?"

"We are far behind you," I answered humbly. "But barbarous as you think we are, no epithet could be too scathing, too comprehensive of all that was vicious and inhuman, to apply to a person who should dare to assail the expense of those institutions, or suggest that they be converted to the cultivation of intellect that *could* be improved."

My friend looked thoughtful for a long time, then she resumed her discourse at the point where I had so unfortunately interrupted it.

"No people," she said, "can rise to universal culture as long as they depend upon hand labor to produce any of the necessities of life. The absence of a demand for hand labor gives rise to an increasing demand for brain labor, and the natural and inevitable result is an increased mental activity. The discovery of a fuel that is furnished at so small a cost and with really no labor but what machinery performs, marks one grand era in our mental progress."

In mentioning the numerous uses made of glass in Mizora, I must not forget to give some notice to their water supply in large cities. Owing to their cleanly advantages, the filtering and storing of rain-water in glass-lined cisterns supplied many family uses. But drinking water was brought to their large cities in a form that did not greatly differ from those I was already familiar with, excepting in cleanliness. Their reservoirs were dug in the ground and lined with glass, and a perfectly fitting cover placed on the top. They were constructed so that the water that passed through the glass feed pipes to the city should have a uniform temperature, that of ordinary spring water. The water in the covered reservoirs was always filtered and tested before passing into the distributing pipes.

No citizen of Mizora ever hied to the country for pure water and fresh air. Science supplied both in a densely populated city.

CHAPTER X.

When a question as to the existence of social distinctions would be asked the citizens of Mizora, the invariable answer would be—there were none; yet a long and intimate acquaintance with them assured me that there were. They had an aristocracy; but of so peculiar and amiable a kind that it deserves a special mention. It took a long time for me to comprehend the exact condition of their society in this respect. That there were really no dividing lines between the person who superintended the kitchen and the one who paid her for it, in a social point of view, I could plainly see; yet there were distinctions; and rather sharply defined ones too.

In order to explain more lucidly the peculiar social life of Mizora, I will ask you to remember some Charity Fair you have attended, perhaps participated in, and which had been gotten up and managed by women of the highest social rank. If in a country where titles and social positions were hereditary, it then represented the highest aristocracy of blood. Grand dames there departed from the routine of their daily lives and assumed the lowlier occupations of others. They stood behind counters, in booths, and sold fancy articles, or dispensed ices and lemonade, or waited upon customers at the refreshment tables; bringing in trays of eatables, gathering up and removing empty dishes; performing labor that, under the ordinary circumstances of life, they would not perform in their own homes, and for their own kindred. It was all done with the same conscious dignity and ease that characterized the statelier duties of their every day life. One fact was apparent to all: they were gentlewomen still. The refinement of their home education, and the charm of nourished beauty were, perhaps, more prominent in contrast with their assumed avocation.

The Charity Fair, with its clerks and waiter girls and flower sellers called from the highest society, was a miniature picture of the actual every-day social life of Mizora. The one who ordered a dinner at their finest hotel, had it served to her by one who occupied the same social standing. Yet there *was* a difference; but it was the difference of mind.

The student in Sociology discovers that in all grades of society, congenial natures gravitate to a center. A differentiation of the highest mental quality was the result of this law in Mizora, and its co-ordinate part, their aristocracy.

The social organism did not need legislation to increase its benefits; it turned to Science, and, through Science, to Nature. The Laboratory of the Chemist was the focus that drew the attention of all minds. Mizora might be called a great school of Nature, whose pupils studied her every phase, and pried into her secrets with persistent activity, and obeyed her instructions as an imperative duty. They observed Nature to be an economist, and practiced economy with scrupulous exactness.

They had observed that in all grades of animal life, from the lowest form to the highest, wherever sociality had produced unity a leader was evolved, a superiority that differed in power according to the grade of development. In the earlier histories, the leaders were chosen for their prowess in arms. Great warriors became rulers, and soldiers were the aristocracy of the land. As civilization progressed and learning became more widely disseminated, the military retired before the more intellectual aristocracy of statemanship. Politics was the grand entrance to social eminence.

"But," said my friend, "*we* have arrived at a higher, nobler, grander age. The military and political supremacies lived out their usefulness and decayed. A new era arrived. The differentia of mind evolved an aristocracy."

Science has long been recognized as the greatest benefactor of our race. Its investigators and teachers are our only acknowledged superiors and leaders.

Generally the grandest intellects and those which retain their creative power the longest, are of exceptionally slow development. Precocity is short lived, and brilliant rather than strong. This I knew to be true of my own race.

In Mizora, a mind that developed late lost none of the opportunities that belong exclusively to the young of my own and other countries of the outer world. Their free schools and colleges were always open: always free. For this reason, it was no unusual thing for a person in Mizora to begin life at the very lowest grade and rise to its supreme height. Whenever the desire awakened, there was a helping hand extended on every side.

The distinction between the aristocracy and the lower class, or the great intellects and the less, was similar to the relative positions of teacher and pupil. I recognized in this social condition the great media of their marvelous approach to perfection. This aristocracy was never arrogant, never supercilious, never aggressive. It was what the philosophers of our world are: tolerant, humane, sublime.

In all communities of civilized nations marked musical talent will form social relations distinct from, but not superior to, other social relations. The leader of a musical club might also be the leader of another club devoted to exclusive literary pursuits; and both clubs possess equal social respect. Those who possess musical predilections, seek musical associations; those who are purely literary, seek their congenials. This is true of all other mental endowments or tastes; that which predominates will seek its affinity; be it in science, literature, politics, music, painting, or sculpture. Social organizations naturally grow out of other business pursuits and vocations of all grades and kinds. The society of Mizora was divided only by such distinctions. The scientific mind had precedence of all others. In the social world, they found more congenial pleasure in one another, and they mingled more frequently among themselves. Other professions and vocations followed their example for the same reason. Yet neither was barred by social caste from seeking society where she would. If the artisan sought social intercourse with a philosopher, she was expected to have prepared herself by mental training to be congenial. When a citizen of Mizora became ambitious to rise, she did not have to struggle with every species of opposition, and contend against rebuff and repulse. Correct language, refined tastes, dignified and graceful manners were the common acquirements of all. Mental culture of so high an order—I marveled that a lifetime should be long enough to acquire it in—was universal.

Under such conditions social barriers could not be impregnable. In a world divided by poverty and opulence into all their intermediate grades, wealth must inevitably be pre-eminent. It represents refined and luxurious environments, and, if mind be there, intellectual pre-eminence also. Where wealth alone governs society it has its prerogatives.

The wealth that affords the most luxurious entertainments must be the wealth that rules. Its privilege—its duty rather—is to ignore all applicants to fraternization that cannot return what it receives. Where mind is the sole aristocracy it makes demands as rigid, though different, and mind was the aristocracy of Mizora. With them education is never at an end. I spoke of having graduated at a renowned school for young ladies, and when I explained that to graduate meant to finish one's education, it elicited a peal of silvery mirth.

" *We* never graduate," said Wauna. "There is my mamma's mother, two centuries old, and still studying. I paid her a visit the other day and she took me into her laboratory. She is a manufacturer of lenses, and has been experimenting on microscopes. She has one now that possesses a truly wonderful power. The leaf of a pear tree, that she had allowed to become mouldy, was under the lens, and she told me to look.

"A panorama of life and activity spread out before me in such magnitude that I can only compare it to the feeling one must possess who could be suspended in air and look down upon our world for a cycle of time.

"Immense plains were visible with animals grazing upon them, that fought with and devoured one another. They perished and sank away and immense forests sprang up like magic. They were inhabited by insects and tiny creatures resembling birds. A sigh of air moved the leaf and a tiny drop of water, scarcely discernible to the naked eye rolled over the forests and plains, and before it passed to the other side of the leaf a great lake covered the spot. My great-great-grandmother has an acute conductor of sound that she has invented, so exquisite in mechanism as to reveal the voice of the tiniest insect. She put it to my ear, and the bellowing of the animals in battle, the chirp of the insects and the voices of the feathered mites could be clearly heard, but attenuated like the delicate note of two threads of spun glass clashed together."

"And what good," I asked, "can all this knowledge do you? Your great-great-grandmother has condensed the learning of two centuries to evolve this one discovery. Is it not so?"

"Yes," replied Wauna, and her look and tone were both solemn. "You ask me what good it can do? Reflect! If the history of a single leaf is so vast and yet ephemeral, what may not be the history of a single world? What, after all, are we when such an infinitesimal space can contain such wonderful transactions in a second of time."

I shuddered at the thought she raised in my mind. But inherited beliefs are not easily dissipated, so I only sought to change the subject.

"But what is the use of studying *all* the time. There should be some period in your lives when you should be permitted to rest from your labors. It is truly irksome to me to see everybody still eager to learn more. The artist of the kitchen was up to the National College yesterday attending a lecture on chemistry. The artist who arranges my rooms is up there to-day listening to one on air. I can not understand why, having learned to make beds and cook to perfection, they should not be content with their knowledge and their work."

"If you were one of us you would know," said Wauna. "It is a duty with us to constantly seek improvement. The culinary artist at the house where you are visiting, is a very fine chemist. She has a predilection for analyzing the construction of food. She may some day discover how *to* produce vegetables from the elements.

"The artist who arranges your room is attending a lecture on air because her vocation calls for an accurate knowledge of it. She attends to the atmosphere in the whole house, and sees that it is in perfect health sustaining condition. Your hostess has a particular fondness for flowers and decorates all her rooms with them. All plants are not harmless occupants of livingrooms. Some give forth exhalations that are really noxious. That artist has so accurate a knowledge of air that she can keep the atmosphere of your home in a condition of perfect purity; yet she knows that her education is not finished. She is constantly studying and advancing. The time may come when she, too, will add a grand discovery to science.

"Had my ancestors thought as you do, and rested on an inferior education, I should not represent the advanced stage of development that I do. As it is, when my mind reaches the age of my mother's, it will have a larger comprehensiveness than hers. She already discerns it. My children will have intellects of a finer grade than mine. This is our system of mind culture. The intellect is of slower development than the body, and takes longer to decay. The gradations of advancement from one intellectual basis to another, in a social body, requires centuries to mark a distinct change in the earlier ages of civilization, but we have now arrived at a stage when advancement is clearly perceptible between one generation and the next."

Wauna's mother added:

"Universal education is the great destroyer of castes. It is the conqueror of poverty and the foundation of patriotism. It purifies and strengthens national, as well as individual character. In the earlier history of our race, there were social conditions that rendered many lives wretched, and that the law would not and, in the then state of civilization, could not reach. They were termed "domestic miseries," and disappeared only under the influence of our higher intellectual development. The nation that is wise will educate its children."

"Alas! alas!" was my own silent thought. "When will my country rise to so grand an idea. When will wealth open the doors of colleges, academies, and schools, and make the Fountain of Knowledge as free as the God-given water we drink."

And there rose a vision in my mind—one of those day dreams when fancy upon the wing takes some definite course—and I saw in my own land a Temple of Learning rise, grand in proportion, complete in detail, with a broad gateway, over whose wide-open majestic portal was the significant inscription: "ENTER WHO WILL: NO WARDER STANDS WATCH AT THE GATE."

CHAPTER XI.

The Government of Mizora not being of primary importance in the estimation of the people, I have not made more than a mere mention of it heretofore. In this respect I have conformed to the generally expressed taste of the Mizora people. In my own country the government and the aristocracy were identical. The government offices and emoluments were the highest pinnacles of ambition.

I mentioned the disparity of opinion between Mizora and all other countries I had known in regard to this. I could not understand why politics in Mizora should be of so small importance. The answer was, that among an educated and highly enlightened people, the government will take care of itself. Having been perfected by wise experience, the people allow it to glide along in the grooves that time has made for it.

In form, the government of Mizora was a Federal Republic. The term of office in no department exceeded the limit of five years. The Presidential term of office was for five years.

They had one peculiar—exceedingly peculiar—law in regard to politics. No candidate could come before the public seeking office before having a certificate from the State College to which she belonged, stating her examination and qualifications to fill such an office.

Just like examining for school-teachers, I thought. And why not? Making laws for a State is of far more importance than making them for a few dozen scholars. I remembered to have heard some of my American acquaintances say that in their country it was not always qualifications that get a candidate into office. Some of the ways were devious and not suitable for publicity. Offices were frequently filled by incompetent men. There had been congressmen and other offices of higher and more responsible duties, filled by persons who could not correctly frame a sentence in their native language, who could not spell the simplest words as they were spelled in the dictionary, unless it were an accident.

To seek the office of President, or any other position under the General Government, required an examination and certificate from the National College. The examinations were always public, and conducted in such a manner that imposture was impossible. Constituents could attend if they chose, and decide upon the qualifications of a favorite candidate. In all the public schools, politics—to a certain extent—formed part of the general education of every child. Beyond that, any one having a predilection for politics could find in the State Colleges and National Colleges the most liberal advantages for acquiring a knowledge of political economy, political arithmetic, and the science of government.

Political campaigns, (if such a term could be applicable to the politics of Mizora) were of the mildest possible character. The papers published the names of the candidates and their examinations in full. The people read and decided upon their choice, and, when the time came, voted. And that was the extent of the campaign enthusiasm.

I must mention that the examinations on the science of government were not conducted as are ordinary examinations in any given study that consists of questions and answers. That was the preliminary part. There followed a thorough, practical test of their ability to discharge the duties of office with wisdom. No matter which side the sympathies or affections might be enlisted upon, the stern decree of justice was what the Mizorean abided by. From earliest infancy their minds were trained in that doctrine. In the discharge of all public duties especially, it seemed to be the paramount consideration. Certainly no government machinery ever could move with more ease, or give greater satisfaction to the people, than that of Mizora.

They never appeared to be excited or uneasy about the result of the elections. I never heard an animated political argument, such as I used to read about in America. I asked a politician one day what she thought of the probable success of the opposite party. She replied that it would not make any difference to the country as both candidates were perfectly competent to fill the office.

"Do you never make disparaging statements about the opposing candidate?" was my inquiry.

"How could we?" she asked in surprise, "when there are none to make."

"You might assume a few for the time being; just to make her lose votes."

"That would be a crime worthy of barbarians."

"Do you never have any party issues?"

"No. There is never anything to make an issue of. We all work for the good of the people, and the whole people. There is no greed of glory or gain; no personal ambition to gratify. Were I to use any artifice to secure office or popularity, I should be instantly deprived of public esteem and notice. I do my duty conscientiously; *that* is the aim of public life. I work for the public good and my popularity comes as it is earned and deserved. I have no fear of being slighted or underrated. Every politician feels and acts the same way."

"Have politicians ever bought votes with money, or offered bribes by promising positions that it would be in their official power to grant when elected?"

"Never! There is not a citizen of Mizora who would not scorn an office obtained in such a way. The profession of politics, while not to be compared in importance with the sciences, is yet not devoid of dignity. It is not necessary to make new laws. They were perfected long ago, and what has been proven good we have no desire to change. We manage the government according to a conscientious interpretation of the law. We have repealed laws that were in force when our Republic was young, and dropped them from the statute books. They were laws unworthy of our civilization. We have laws for the protection of property and to regulate public morals, and while our civilization is in a state of advancement that does not require them, yet we think it wisdom to let them remain. The people know that we have such laws and live up to them without surveillance. They would abide by the principles of justice set forth in them just as scrupulously if we should repeal them.

"You spoke of bribes. In remote ages, when our country was emerging from a state of semi-barbarism, such things were in common practice. Political chicanery was a name given to various underhand and dishonest maneuvers to gain office and public power. It was frequently the case that the most responsible positions in the Government would be occupied by the basest characters, who used their power only for fraud to enrich themselves and their friends by robbing the people. They deceived the masses by preaching purity. They were never punished. If they were accused and brought to trial, the wealth they had stolen from the government purchased their acquittal, and then they posed as martyrs. The form of government was then, as now, a Federal Republic, but the people had very little to do with it. They were merely the tools of unscrupulous politicians. In those days a sensitively honest person would not accept office, because the name politician was a synonym for flexible principles. It was derogatory to one's character to seek office."

"Was dishonesty more prominent in one party than another?" I asked, thinking how very Americanish this history sounded.

"We, who look back upon the conditions of those times and view it with dispassionate judgment, can perceive corruption in both political parties. The real welfare of the country was the last thing considered by a professional politician. There was always something that was to benefit the people brought forward as a party issue, and used as a means of working up the enthusiasm or fears of the people, and usually dropped after the election.

"The candidate for election in those days might be guilty of heinous crimes, yet the party covered them all, and over that covering the partisan newspaper spread every virtue in the calendar. A stranger to the country and its customs reading one of their partisan newspapers during a political campaign, might conclude that the party *it* advocated was composed of only the virtues of the country, and their leader an epitome of the supremest excellence.

"Reading in the same paper a description of the opposing party, the stranger might think it composed of only the degraded and disreputable portion of the nation, and its leader the scum of all its depravity. If curiosity should induce a perusal of some partisan paper of the other party, the same thing could be read in its columns, with a change of names. It would be the opposite party that was getting represented in the most despicable character, and *their* leader was the only one who possessed enough honesty and talent to keep the country from going to wreck. The other party leader was the one who was guilty of all the crimes in the calendar. A vast number of people were ignorant enough to cling blindly to one party and to believe every word published by its partisan papers. This superstitious party faith was what the unscrupulous politicians handled dexterously for their own selfish ends. It was not until education became universal, and a higher culture was forced upon the majority—the working classes—that politics began to purify itself, and put on the dignity of real virtue, and receive the respect that belongs to genuine justice.

"The people became disgusted with defamatory political literature, and the honorable members of both parties abjured it altogether. In such a government as this, two great parties could not exist, where one was altogether bad and the other altogether good. It became apparent to the people that there was good in both parties, and they began to elect it irrespective of party prejudice. Politicians began to work for their country instead of themselves and their party, and politics took the noble position that the rights of humanity designed it for. I have been giving you quite a history of our ancient politics. Our present condition is far different. As the people became enlightened to a higher degree, the government became more compact. It might now be compared to a large family. There are one hundred States in the Union. There was a time when every State made its own laws for its own domestic government. One code of laws is now enforced in every State. In going from one State to another citizens now suffer no inconvenience from a confusion of laws. Every State owes allegiance to the General Government. No State or number of States could set up an independent government without obtaining the consent and legal dissolution from the General Government. But such a thing will never be thought of. We have prospered as a great united Nation. Our union has been our strength, our prosperity."

I visited with Wauna a number of the States' Capitals. In architecture the Mizora people display an excellent taste. Their public buildings might all be called works of art. Their government buildings, especially, were on a scale of magnificent splendor. The hollow square seemed to be a favorite form. One very beautiful capitol building was of crystal glass, with facing and cornices of marble onyx. It looked more like a gigantic gem than anything I could compare it to, especially when lighted up by great globes of white fire suspended from every ceiling.

Upon my entrance into Mizora, I was led into the belief that I had arrived at a female seminary, because the dining and sleeping accommodations for the stateswoman were all in the Capitol building. I observed that the State Capitols were similarly accommodated. In Mizora the home is the heart of all joy, and wherever a Mizora woman goes, she endeavors to surround herself with its comforts and pleasures. That was the reason that the splendid Capitol building had its home-like appointments, was a Nation of women exclusively—at least as far as I had as yet been able to discover.

Another reason for the homes of all officials of the Government being within the public buildings, was because all the personal expenses, excepting clothing, were paid by the Government. The salaries of Government positions were not large, compared with those of the sciences; but as their social and political dues were paid out of the public treasury, the salaries might be considered as net profit. This custom had originated many centuries in the past. In those early days, when a penurious character became an incumbent of public office, the social obligations belonging to it were often but niggardly requited. Sometimes business embarrassments and real necessity demanded economy; so, at last, the Government assumed all the expenses contingent upon every office, from the highest to the lowest. By this means the occupant of a Government office was freed from every care but those of state.

The number and style of all social entertainments that were obligatory of the occupant of a public office, were regulated by law. As the people of Mizora believed in enjoyment, the entertainments provided by the Government as the necessary social dues of its officers, were not few, nor scantily furnished.

CHAPTER XII.

The artificial light in Mizora puzzled me longest to understand. When I first noticed it, it appeared to me to have no apparent source. At the touch of a delicate hand, it blazed forth like a star in the center of the ceiling. It diffused a soft and pleasing brilliancy that lent a charm to everything it revealed. It was a dreamy daylight, and was produced by electricity.

In large halls, like a theatre or opera house, the light fell in a soft and penetrating radiance from the center of the dome. Its source was not visible to either audience or actresses, and, in consequence, occasioned no discomfort to the eyes. The light that illuminated the stage was similarly arranged. The footlights were not visible. They were in the rear of the stage. The light came upward like the rays of the setting sun, revealing the setting of the stage with vivid distinctness. I can best describe the effect of this singular arrangement by calling attention to the appearance of the sun when declining behind a small elevation. How sharply every object is outlined before it? How soft and delicate is the light in which everything is bathed? Every cloud that floats has all of its fleecy loveliness limned with a radiant clearness.

I was very desirous to know how this singular effect was produced, and at my request was taken to the stage. An opening in the back part of it was covered with pink colored glass. Powerful electric lights from below the stage were reflected through this glass upon it. The glass was highly refractive and so perfectly translucent, I at first thought there was none there, and when I stood upon its edge, and looked down into a fiery gulf below, I instinctively thought of the "Lost People," who are said to wander amid torturing yet unconsumable flames. But, happily, the ones I gazed upon were harmless ones.

The street lights of Mizora were at a considerable elevation from the ground. They were in, or over, the center of the street, and of such diffuse brilliancy as to render the city almost as light as day. They were in the form of immense globes of soft, white fire, and during the six months that answered to the Mizora night, were kept constantly burning. It was during this period that the Aurora Borealis shone with such marvelous brilliancy.

Generally, its display was heralded by an arc of delicate green-tinted light, that spanned the heavens. The green tint deepened into emerald, assuming a delicate rose hue as it faded upward into rays that diverged from the top until the whole resembled a gigantic crown. Every ray became a panorama of gorgeous colors, resembling tiny sparks, moving hither and thither with inconceivable swiftness. Sometimes a veil of mist of delicate green hue depended from the base of the crown, and swayed gently back and forth. As soon as the swaying motion commenced, the most gorgeous colors were revealed. Myriads of sparks, no larger than snow-flakes, swarmed across the delicate green curtain in every conceivable color and shade, but always of that vapory, vivid softness that is indescribable. The dancing colors resembled gems encased in a film of mist.

One display that I witnessed I shall attempt to describe. The arc of delicate green appeared first, and shot upward diverging rays of all the warm, rich hues of red. They formed a vast crown, outlined with a delicate halo of fire. A veil of misty green fluttered down from its base, and, instantly, tiny crowns, composed of every brilliant color, with a tracery of fire defining every separate one, began to chase one another back and forth with bewildering rapidity. As the veil swayed to and fro, it seemed to shake the crowns into skeins of fire, each thread strung with countless minute globes of every conceivable color and hue. Those fiery threads, aerial as thistle down, wove themselves in and out in a tangled mass of gorgeous beauty. Suddenly the beads of color fell in a shower of gems, topaz and emerald, ruby and sapphire, amethyst and pearly crystals of dew. I looked upward, where the rays of variegated colors were sweeping the zenith, and high above the first crown was a second more vivid still. Myriads of rainbows, the colors broad and intense, fluttered from its base, the whole outlined by a halo of fire. It rolled together in a huge scroll, and, in an instant, fell apart a shower of flakes, minute as snow, but of all the gorgeous, dazzling hues of earth and sky combined. They disappeared in the mystery of space to instantly form into a fluttering, waving banner of delicate green mist and—vanish; only to repeat itself.

The display of the Aurora Borealis was always an exhibition of astonishing rapidity of motion of intense colors. The most glorious sunset—where the vapory billows of the sky have caught the bloom of the dying Autumn—cannot rival it. All the precious gems of earth appear to have dissolved into mist, to join in a wild and aerial dance. The people of Mizora attributed it entirely to electricity.

Although the sun never rose or set in Mizora, yet for six months in a year, that country had the heart of a voluptuous summer. It beat with a strong, warm pulse of life through all nature. The orchards budded and bloomed, and mellowed into perfect fruition their luscious globes. The fields laughed in the warm, rich light, and smiled on the harvest. I could feel my own blood bound as with a new lease of life at the first breath of spring.

The winters of Mizora had clouds and rain and sleet and snow, and sometimes, especially near the circular sea, the fury of an Arctic snow storm; but so well prepared were they that it became an amusement. Looking into the chaos of snow flakes, driven hither and thither by fierce winds, the pedestrians in the street presented no painful contrast to the luxury of your own room, with its balmy breath and cheerful flowers. You saw none but what were thoroughly clad, and you knew that they were hurrying to homes that were bright and attractive, if not as elegant as yours; where loving welcomes were sure to greet them and happiness would sit with them at the feast; for the heart that is pure has always a kingly guest for its company.

A wonderful discovery that the people of Mizora had made was the power to annihilate space as an impediment to conversation. They claimed that the atmosphere had regular currents of electricity that were accurately known to them. They talked to them by means of simply constructed instruments, and the voice would be as audible and as easily recognized at three thousand miles distant as at only three feet. Stations were built similar to our telegraph offices, but on high elevations. I understood that they could not be used upon the surface. Every private and public house, however, had communication with the general office, and could converse with friends at a distance whenever desirable. Public speakers made constant use of it, but in connection with another extraordinary apparatus which I regret my inability to perfectly describe.

I saw it first from the dress circle of a theater. It occupied the whole rear of the stage, and from where I sat, looked like a solid wall of polished metal. But it had a wonderful function, for immediately in front of it, moving, speaking and gesturing, was the figure of a popular public lecturer, so life-like in appearance that I could scarcely be convinced that it was only a reflection. Yet such it was, and the original was addressing an audience in person more than a thousand miles distant.

It was no common thing for a lecturer to address a dozen or more audiences at the same time, scattered over an area of thousands of miles, and every one listening to and observing what appeared to be the real speaker. In fact, public speakers in Mizora never traveled on pure professional business. It was not necessary. They prepared a room in their own dwelling with the needful apparatus, and at the time specified delivered a lecture in twenty different cities.

I was so interested in this very remarkable invention that I made vigorous mental exertions to comprehend it sufficiently to explain its mechanism and philosophical principles intelligently; but I can only say that it was one of the wonders those people produced with electricity. The mechanism was simple, but the science of its construction and workings I could not comprehend. The grasp of my mind was not broad enough. The instrument that transmitted the voice was entirely separate.

I must not neglect to mention that all kinds of public entertainments, such as operas, concerts and dramas, could be and were repeated to audiences at a distance from where the real transaction was taking place. I attended a number of operas that were only the reflex of others that were being presented to audiences far distant.

These repetitions were always marvels of accuracy of vividness.

Small reflecting apparatus were to be found in every dwelling and business house. It is hardly necessary to state that letter-writing was an unknown accomplishment in Mizora. The person who desired to converse with another, no matter how far distant, placed herself in communication with her two instruments and signaled. Her friend appeared upon the polished metal surface like the figure in a mirror, and spoke to her audibly, and looked at her with all the naturalness of reality.

I have frequently witnessed such interviews between Wauna and her mother, when we were visiting distant cities. It was certainly a more satisfactory way of communicating than by letter. The small apparatus used by private families and business houses were not like those used in public halls and theaters. In the former, the reflection was exactly similar to the image of a mirror; in the latter, the figure was projected upon the stage. It required more complicated machinery to produce, and was not practicable for small families or business houses. I now learned that on my arrival in Mizora I had been taken to one of the largest apparatus and put in communication with it. I was informed by Wauna that I had been exhibited to every college and school in the country by reflex representation. She said that she and her mother had seen me distinctly and heard my voice. The latter had been so uncongenial in accent and tone that she had hesitated about becoming my instructor on that account. It was my evident appreciation of my deficiencies as compared to them that had enlisted her sympathy.

Now, in my own country, my voice had attracted attention by its smoothness and modulation, and I was greatly surprised to hear Wauna speak of its unmusical tone as really annoying. But then in Mizora there are no voices but what are sweet enough to charm the birds.

In the journeys that Wauna and I took during the college vacation, we were constantly meeting strangers, but they never appeared the least surprised at my dark hair and eyes, which were such a contrast to all the other hair and eyes to be met with in Mizora, that I greatly wondered at it until I learned of the power of the reflector. I requested permission to examine one of the large ones used in a theater, and it was granted me. Wauna accompanied me and signaled to a friend of hers. As if by magic a form appeared and moved across the stage. It bowed to me, smiled and motioned with its hand, to all appearances a material body. I asked Wauna to approach it, which she did, and passed her hand through it. There was nothing that resisted her touch, yet I plainly saw the figure, and recognized it as the perfect representation of a friend of Wauna's, an actress residing in a distant city. When I ascended the stage, the figure vanished, and I understood that it could be visible only at a certain distance from the reflector.

In traveling great distances, or even short ones where great speed was desired, the Mizoraens used air ships; but only for the transportation of passengers and the very lightest of freight. Heavy articles could not be as conveniently carried by them as by railroads. Their railroads were constructed and conducted on a system so perfect that accidents were never known. Every engineer had an electric signal attached to the engine, that could signal a train three miles distant.

The motive power for nearly all engines was compressed air. Electricity, which was recognized by Mizora scientists as a force of great intensity, was rarely used as a propelling power on railroads. Its use was attended by possible danger, but compressed air was not. Electricity produced the heat that supplied the air ships and railroads with that very necessary comfort. In case there should be an accident, as a collision, or thrown from the track, heat could not be a source of danger when furnished by electricity. But I never heard of a railroad accident during the whole fifteen years that I spent in Mizora.

Air-ships, however, were not exempt from danger, although the precautions against it were ingenious and carefully observed. The Mizora people could tell the approach of a storm, and the exact time it would arrive. They had signal stations established for the purpose, all over the country.

But, though they were skilled mechanics, and far in advance of my own world, and the limits of my comprehension in their scientific discoveries and appliances, they had not yet discovered the means of subduing the elements, or driving unharmed through their fury. When nature became convulsed with passion, they guarded themselves against it, but did not endeavor to thwart it.

Their air-ships were covered, and furnished with luxurious seats. The whole upper part of the car was composed of very thin glass. They traveled with, to me, astonishing rapidity. Towns and cities flew away beneath us like birds upon the wing. I grew frightened and apprehensive, but Wauna chatted away with her friends with the most charming unconcern.

I was looking down, when I perceived, by the increasing size of objects below, that we were descending. The conductor entered almost immediately, and announced that we were going down to escape an approaching storm. A signal had been received and the ship was at once lowered.

I felt intensely relieved to step again on solid earth, and hoped I might escape another trial of the upper regions. But after waiting until the storm was over we again entered the ship. I was ashamed to refuse when everyone else showed no fear.

In waiting for the storm to pass we were delayed so long that our journey could have been performed almost as speedily by rail. I wondered why they had not invented some means by which they could drive through a tempest in perfect safety. As usual, I addressed my inquiries to Wauna. She answered:

"So frail a thing as an air-ship must necessarily be, when compared with the strength of a storm, is like a leaf in the wind. We have not yet discovered, and we have but little expectation of discovering, any means by which we can defy the storms that rage in the upper deeps.

"The electricity that we use for heat is also a source of danger during a storm. Our policy is to evade a peril we cannot control or destroy. Hence, when we receive a signal that a storm is approaching we get out of its way. Our railroad carriages, having no danger to fear from them, ride right through the storm."

The people of Mizora, I perceived, possessed a remarkable acuteness of vision. They could see the odor emanating from flowers and fruit. They described it to me as resembling attenuated mist. They also named other colors in the solar spectrum than those known to me. When I first heard them speak of them, I thought it a freak of the imagination; but I afterward noticed artists, and persons who had a special taste for colors, always detected them with greater readiness. The presence of these new colors were apparent to all with whom I spoke upon the subject. When I mentioned my own inability to discern them, Wauna said that it was owning to my inferior mental development.

"A child," she said, "if you will observe, is first attracted by red, the most glaring color known. The untutored mind will invariably select the gaudiest colors for personal adornment. It is the gentle, refined taste of civilization that chooses the softened hues and colors."

"But you, as a nation, are remarkable for rich warm colors in your houses and often in your dress," I said.

"But they are never glaring," she replied. "If you will notice, the most intense colors are always so arranged as to present a halo, instead of sharply defined brilliancy. If a gorgeous color is worn as a dress, it will be covered with filmy lace. You have spoken of the splendor of the Aurora Borealis. It is nature's most gorgeous robe, and intense as the primal colors are, they are never glaring. They glow in a film of vapor. We have made them our study. Art, with us, has never attempted to supercede nature."

The sense of smell was also exceedingly sensitive with the Mizora people. They detected odors so refined that I was not aware of them. I have often seen a chemist take a bottle of perfumery and name its ingredients from the sense of smell only. No one appeared surprised at the bluntness of my senses. When I spoke of this Wauna tried to explain it.

"We are a more delicately organized race of beings than you are. Our intellects, and even sense that we possess, is of a higher and finer development. We have some senses that you do not possess, and are unable to comprehend their exquisite delicacy. One of them I shall endeavor to explain to you by describing it as impression. We possess it in a highly refined state, both mentally and physically. Our sensitiveness to changes of temperature, I have noticed, is more marked than yours. It is acute with all of my people. For this reason, although we are free from disease, our bodies could not sustain, as readily as yours could, a sudden and severe shock to their normal temperature, such as a marked change in the atmosphere would occasion. We are, therefore, extremely careful to be always appropriately clothed. That is a physical impression. It is possessed by you also, but more obtusely.

"Our sensitiveness to mental pleasure and pain you would pronounce morbid on account of its intensity. The happiness we enjoy in the society of those who are congenial, or near and dear to us through family ties, is inconceivable to you. The touch of my mother's hand carries a thrill of rapture with it.

"We feel, intuitively, the happiness or disappointment of those we are with. Our own hopes impress us with their fulfillment or frustration, before we know what will actually occur. This feeling is entirely mental, but it is evidence of a highly refined mentality. We could not be happy unless surrounded, as we are, by cultivated and elegant pleasures. They are real necessities to us.

"Our appreciation of music, I notice, has a more exquisite delicacy than yours. You desire music, but it is the simpler operas that delight you most. Those fine and delicate harmonies that we so intensely enjoy, you appear incapable of appreciating."

I have previously spoken of their elegance in dress, and their fondness for luxury and magnificence. On occasions of great ceremony their dresses were furnished with very long trains. The only prominent difference that I saw in their state dresses, and the rare and costly ones I had seen in my own and other countries, was in the waist. As the women of Mizora admired a large waist, their dresses were generally loose and flowing. Ingenuity, however, had fashioned them into graceful and becoming outlines. On occasions of great state and publicity, comfortably fitting girdles confined the dress at the waist.

I attended the Inaugural of a Professor of Natural History in the National College. The one who had succeeded to this honor was widely celebrated for her erudition. It was known that the ceremony would be a grand affair, and thousands attended it.

I there witnessed another of these marvelous achievements in science that were constantly surprising me in Mizora. The inauguration took place in a large hall, the largest I had ever seen. It would accommodate two hundred thousand people, and was filled to repletion. I was seated far back in the audience, and being a little short-sighted anyway, I expected to be disappointed both in seeing and hearing the ceremonies. What was my astonishment then, when they began, to discover that I could see distinctly every object upon the stage, and hear with perfect accuracy every word that was uttered.

Upon expressing myself to Wauna as being greatly pleased that my eyesight and hearing had improved so wonderfully and unexpectedly, she laughed merrily, and asked me if I had noticed a curious looking band of polished steel that curved outward from the proscenium, and encircled its entire front? I had noticed it, but supposed it to be connected with some different arrangement they might have made concerning the footlights. Wauna informed me that I owed my improved hearing to that.

"But my eyesight," I asked, "how do you account for its unusual penetrativeness?"

"Have you ever noticed some seasons of the year display a noticeably marked transparency of the atmosphere that revealed objects at great distances with unusual clearness? Well, we possess a knowledge of air that enables us to qualify it with that peculiar magnifying condition. On occasions like this we make use of it. This hall was built after the discovery, and was specially prepared for its use. It is seldom employed in smaller halls."

Just then a little flutter of interest upon the stage attracted my attention, and I saw the candidate for the professorship entering, accompanied by the Faculty of the National College.

She wore a sea-green velvet robe with a voluminous train. The bottom of the dress was adorned with a wreath or band of water lilies, embroidered in seed pearls. A white lace overdress of filmiest texture fell over the velvet, almost touching the wreath of lilies, and looked as though it was made of sea foam. A girdle of large pink pearls confined the robe at the waist. Natural flowers were on her bosom and in her hair.

The stage was superbly decorated with flowers and shells. A large chair, constructed of beautiful shells and cushioned with green velvet, rested upon a dais of coral. It was the chair of honor. Behind it was a curtain of sea-moss. I afterward learned that the moss was attached to a film of glass too delicate to detect without handling.

In the midst of these charming surroundings stood the applicant for honor. Her deep blue eyes glowed with the joy of triumph. On the delicate cheek and lip burned the carmine hue of perfect health. The golden hair even seemed to have caught a brighter lustre in its coiled masses. The uplifted hand and arm no marble goddess could have matched, for this had the color and charm of life. As she stood revealed by the strong light that fell around her, every feature ennobled with the glory of intellect, she appeared to me a creature of unearthly loveliness, as something divine.

I spoke to Wauna of the rare beauty and elegance of her dress.

"She looks like a fabled Naiad just risen from the deep," was my criticism on her.

"Her dress," answered Wauna, "is intended to be emblematical of Nature. The sea-green robe, the water lilies of pearls, the foamy lace are all from Nature's Cradle of Life."

"How poetical!" I exclaimed.

But then Mizora is full of that charming skill that blends into perfect harmony the beautiful and useful in life.

CHAPTER XIII.

On my return to college, after the close of vacation, I devoted myself exclusively to history. It began with their first President; and from the evidence of history itself, I knew that the Nation was enjoying a high state of culture when its history began.

No record of a more primitive race was to be found in all the Library, assiduously as I searched for it. I read with absorbing interest their progress toward perfect enlightenment, their laborious searchings into science that had resulted in such marvelous achievements. But earnestly as I sought for it, and anxiously as I longed for it, I found and heard no mention of a race of men. From the most intimate intercourse with the people of Mizora, I could discover no attempt at concealment in anything, yet the inquiry *would* crowd itself upon me. "Where are the men?" And as constantly would I be forced to the conclusion that Mizora was either a land of mystery beyond the scope of the wildest and weirdest fancy, or else they were utterly oblivious of such a race. And the last conclusion was most improbable of all.

Man, in my country, was a necessity of government, law, and protection. His importance, (as I viewed it from inherited ideas) was incalculable. It *could* not be possible that he had no existence in a country so eminently adapted to his desires and ability.

The expression, "domestic misery," that the Preceptress made use of one day in conversation with me, haunted my imagination with a persistent suspicion of mystery. It had a familiar sound to me. It intimated knowledge of a world *I* knew so well; where ill-nature, malice, spite, envy, deceit, falsehood and dishonesty, made life a continual anxiety.

Locks, bolts and bars shut out the thief who coveted your jewels; but no bolts nor bars, however ingeniously constructed or strongly made, could keep out the thief who coveted your character. One little word from a pretended friend might consummate the sorrow of your whole life, and be witnessed by the perpetrator without a pang— nay, even with exultation.

There were other miseries I thought of that were common in my country. There were those we love. Some who are woven into our lives and affections by the kinship of blood; who grow up weak and vacillating, and are won away, sometimes through vice, to estrangement. Our hearts ache not the less painfully that they have ceased to be worthy of a throb; or that they have been weak enough to become estranged, to benefit some selfish alien.

There were other sorrows in that world that I had come from, that brought anguish alike to the innocent and the guilty. It was the sorrow of premature death. Diseases of all kinds made lives wretched; or tore them asunder with death. How many hearts have ached with cankering pain to see those who are vitally dear, wasting away slowly, but surely, with unrelievable suffering; and to know that life but prolongs their misery, and death relieves it only with inconsolable grief for the living.

Who has looked into a pair of youthful eyes, so lovely that imagination could not invent for them another charm, and saw the misty film of death gather over them, while your heart ached with regret as bitter as it was unavailing. The soft snows of winter have fallen—a veil of purity—over the new made graves of innocence and youth, and its wild winds have been the saddest requiem. The dews of summer have wept with your tears, and its zephyrs have sighed over the mouldering loveliness of youth.

I had known no skill in my world that could snatch from death its unlawful prey of youth. But here, in this land so eminently blessed, no one regarded death as a dreaded invader of their household.

"*We cannot die until we get old*," said Wauna, naively.

And looking upon their bounding animal spirits, their strong supple frames, and the rich, red blood of perfect health, mantling their cheeks with its unsurpassable bloom, one would think that disease must have strong grasp indeed that could destroy them.

But these were not all the sorrows that my own country knew. Crimes, with which we had no personal connection, shocked us with their horrible details. They crept, like noxious vapors, into the moral atmosphere of the pure and good; tainting the weak, and annoying the strong.

There were other sorrows in my country that were more deplorable still. It was the fate of those who sought to relieve the sufferings of the many by an enforced government reform. Misguided, imprudent and fanatical they might be, but their aim at least was noble. The wrongs and sufferings of the helpless and oppressed had goaded them to action for their relief.

But, alas! The pale and haggard faces of thousands of those patriot souls faded and wasted in torturing slowness in dungeons of rayless gloom. Or their emaciated and rheumatic frames toiled in speechless agony amid the horrors of Siberia's mines.

In *this* land they would have been recognized as aspiring natures, spreading their wings for a nobler flight, seeking a higher and grander life. The smile of beauty would have urged them on. Hands innumerable would have given them a cordial and encouraging grasp. But in the land they had sought to benefit and failed, they suffered in silence and darkness, and died forgotten or cursed.

My heart and my brain ached with memory, and the thought again occurred: "*Could* the Preceptress ever have known such a race of people?"

I looked at her fair, calm brow, where not a wrinkle marred the serene expression of intellect, although I had been told that more than a hundred years had touched with increasing wisdom its broad surface. The smile that dwelt in her eyes, like the mystic sprite in the fountain, had not a suspicion of sadness in them. A nature so lofty as hers, where every feeling had a generous and noble existence and aim, could not have known without anguish the race of people *I* knew so well. Their sorrows would have tinged her life with a continual sadness.

The words of Wauna had awakened a new thought. I knew that their mental life was far above mine, and that in all the relations of life, both business and social, they exhibited a refinement never attained by my people. I had supposed these qualities to be an endowment of nature, and not a development sought and labored for by themselves. But my conversation with Wauna had given me a different impression, and the thought of a future for my own country took possession of me.

"Could it ever emerge from its horrors, and rise through gradual but earnest endeavor to such perfection? Could a higher civilization crowd its sufferings out of existence and, in time, memory?"

I had never thought of my country having a claim upon me other than what I owed to my relatives and society. But in Mizora, where the very atmosphere seemed to feed one's brain with grander and nobler ideas of life and humanity, my nature had drank the inspiration of good deeds and impulses, and had given the desire to work for something beside myself and my own kindred. I resolved that if I should ever again behold my native country, I would seek the good of all its people along with that of my nearest and dearest of kin. But how to do it was a matter I could not arrange. I felt reluctant to ask either Wauna or her mother. The guileless frankness of Wauna's nature was an impassable barrier to the confidence of crimes and wretchedness. One glance of horror from her dark, sweet eyes, would have chilled me into painful silence and sorrowful regret.

The mystery that had ever surrounded these lovely and noble blonde women had driven me into an unnatural reserve in regard to my own people and country. I had always perceived the utter absence of my allusion to the masculine gender, and conceiving that it must be occasioned by some more than ordinary circumstances, I refrained from intruding my curiosity.

That the singular absence of men was connected with nothing criminal or ignoble on their part I felt certain; but that it was associated with something weird and mysterious I had now become convinced. My efforts to discover their whereabouts had been earnest and untiring. I had visited a number of their large cities, and had enjoyed the hospitality of many private homes. I had examined every nook and corner of private and public buildings, (for in Mizora nothing ever has locks) and in no place had I ever discovered a trace or suggestion of man.

Women and girls were everywhere. Their fair faces and golden heads greeted me in every town and city. Sometimes a pair of unusually dark blue eyes, like the color of a velvet-leaved pansy, looked out from an exquisitely tinted face framed in flossy golden hair, startling me with its unnatural loveliness, and then I would wonder anew:

"Why is such a paradise for man so entirely devoid of him?"

I even endeavored to discover from the conversation of young girls some allusion to the male sex. But listen as attentively and discreetly as I could, not one allusion did I hear made to the mysteriously absent beings. I was astonished that young girls, with cheeks like the downy bloom of a ripe peach, should chatter and laugh merrily over every conversational topic but that of the lords of society. The older and the wiser among women might acquire a depreciating idea of their worth, but innocent and inexperienced girlhood was apt to surround that name with a halo of romance and fancied nobility that the reality did not always possess. What, then, was my amazement to find *them* indifferent and wholly neglectful of that (to me) very important class of beings.

Conjecture at last exhausted itself, and curiosity became indifferent. Mizora, as a nation, or an individual representative, was incapable of dishonor. Whatever their secret I should make no farther effort to discover it. Their hospitality had been generous and unreserved. Their influence upon my character—morally—had been an incalculable benefit. I had enjoyed being among them. The rhythm of happiness that swept like a strain of sweet music through all their daily life, touched a chord in my own nature that responded.

And when I contrasted the prosperity of Mizora—a prosperity that reached every citizen in its vast territory—with the varied phases of life that are found in my own land, it urged me to inquire if there could be hope for such happiness within its borders.

To the Preceptress, whose sympathies I knew were broad as the lap of nature, I at last went with my desire and perplexities. A sketch of my country's condition was the inevitable prelude. I gave it without once alluding to the presence of Man. She listened quietly and attentively. Her own land lay like a charming picture before her. I spoke of its peaceful happiness, its perfected refinement, its universal wealth, and paramount to all its other blessings, its complete ignorance of social ills. With them, love did not confine itself to families, but encircled the Nation in one embrace. How dismal, in contrast, was the land that had given me birth.

"But one eminent distinction exists among us as a people," I added in conclusion. "We are not all of one race."

I paused and looked at the Preceptress. She appeared lost in reverie. Her expression was one of solicitude and approached nearer to actual pain than anything I had ever noticed upon it before. She looked up and caught my eye regarding her. Then she quietly asked:

"*Are there men in your country?*"

PART SECOND   CHAPTER I.

I answered in the affirmative, and further added that I had a husband and a son.

The effect of a confession so simple, and so natural, wounded and amazed me.

The Preceptress started back with a look of loathing and abhorrence; but it was almost instantly succeeded by one of compassion.

"You have much to learn," she said gently, "and I desire not to judge you harshly. *You* are the product of a people far back in the darkness of civilization. *We* are a people who have passed beyond the boundary of what was once called Natural Law. But, more correctly, we have become mistresses of Nature's peculiar processes. We influence or control them at will. But before giving you any further explanation I will show you the gallery containing the portraits of our very ancient ancestors."

She then conducted me into a remote part of the National College, and sliding back a panel containing a magnificent painting, she disclosed a long gallery, the existence of which I had never suspected, although I knew their custom of using ornamented sliding panels instead of doors. Into this I followed her with wonder and increasing surprise. Paintings on canvas, old and dim with age; paintings on porcelain, and a peculiar transparent material, of which I have previously spoken, hung so thick upon the wall you could not have placed a hand between them. They were all portraits of men. Some were represented in the ancient or mediaeval costumes of my own ancestry, and some in garbs resembling our modern styles.

Some had noble countenances, and some bore on their painted visages the unmistakable stamp of passion and vice. It is not complimentary to myself to confess it, but I began to feel an odd kind of companionship in this assembly of good and evil looking men, such as I had not felt since entering this land of pre-eminently noble and lovely women.

As I gazed upon them, arrayed in the armor of some stern warrior, or the velvet doublet of some gay cavalier, the dark eyes of a debonair knight looked down upon me with familiar fellowship. There was pride of birth, and the passion of conquest in every line of his haughty, sensuous face. I seemed to breathe the same moral atmosphere that had surrounded me in the outer world.

They had lived among noble and ignoble deeds I felt sure. *They* had been swayed by conflicting desires. *They* had known temptation and resistance, and reluctant compliance. *They* had experienced the treachery and ingratitude of humanity, and had dealt in it themselves. *They* had known joy as I had known it, and their sorrow had been as my sorrows. *They* had loved as I had loved, and sinned as I had sinned, and suffered as I had suffered.

I wept for the first time since my entrance into Mizora, the bitter tears of actual experience, and endeavored to convey to the Preceptress some idea of the painful emotion that possessed me.

"I have noticed," she said, "in your own person and the descriptions you have given of your native country, a close resemblance to the people and history of our nation in ages far remote. These portraits are very old. The majority of them were painted many thousands of years ago. It is only by our perfect knowledge of color that we are enabled to preserve them. Some have been copied by expert artists upon a material manufactured by us for that purpose. It is a transparent adamant that possesses no refractive power, consequently the picture has all the advantage of a painting on canvas, with the addition of perpetuity. They can never fade nor decay."

"I am astonished at the existence of this gallery," I exclaimed. "I have observed a preference for sliding panels instead of doors, and that they were often decorated with paintings of rare excellence, but I had never suspected the existence of this gallery behind one of them."

"Any student," said the Preceptress, "who desires to become conversant with our earliest history, can use this gallery. It is not a secret, for nothing in Mizora is concealed; but we do not parade its existence, nor urge upon students an investigation of its history. They are so far removed from the moral imbecility that dwarfed the nature of these people, that no lesson can be learned from their lives; and their time can be so much more profitably spent in scientific research and study."

"You have not, then, reached the limits of scientific knowledge?" I wonderingly inquired, for, to me, they had already overstepped its imaginary pale.

"When we do we shall be able to create intellect at will. We govern to a certain extent the development of physical life; but the formation of the brain—its intellectual force, or capacity I should say—is beyond our immediate skill. Genius is yet the product of long cultivation."

I had observed that dark hair and eyes were as indiscriminately mingled in these portraits as I had been accustomed to find them in the living people of my own and other countries. I drew the Preceptress' attention to it.

"We believe that the highest excellence of moral and mental character is alone attainable by a fair race. The elements of evil belong to the dark race."

"And were the people of this country once of mixed complexions?"

"As you see in the portraits? Yes," was the reply.

"And what became of the dark complexions?"

"We eliminated them."

I was too astonished to speak and stood gazing upon the handsome face of a young man in a plumed hat and lace-frilled doublet. The dark eyes had a haughty look, like a man proud of his lineage and his sex.

"Let us leave this place," said the Preceptress presently. "It always has a depressing effect upon me."

"In what way?" I asked.

"By the degradation of the human race that they force me to recall."

I followed her out to a seat on one of the small porticoes.

In candidly expressing herself about the dark complexions, my companion had no intention or thought of wounding my feelings. So rigidly do they adhere to the truth in Mizora that it is of all other things pre-eminent, and is never supposed to give offense. The Preceptress but gave expression to the belief inculcated by centuries of the teachings and practices of her ancestors. I was not offended. It was her conviction. Besides, I had the consolation of secretly disagreeing with her. I am still of the opinion that their admirable system of government, social and political, and their encouragement and provision for universal culture of so high an order, had more to do with the formation of superlative character than the elimination of the dark complexion.

The Preceptress remained silent a long time, apparently absorbed in the beauty of the landscape that stretched before us. The falling waters of a fountain was all the sound we heard. The hour was auspicious. I was so eager to develop a revelation of the mystery about these people that I became nervous over my companion's protracted silence. I felt a delicacy in pressing inquiries concerning information that I thought ought to be voluntarily given. Inquisitiveness was regarded as a gross rudeness by them, and I could frame no question that I did not fear would sound impertinent. But at last patience gave way and, at the risk of increasing her commiseration for my barbarous mental condition, I asked:

"Are you conversant with the history of the times occupied by the originals of the portraits we have just seen?"

"I am," she replied.

"And would you object to giving me a condensed recital of it?"

"Not if it can do you any good?"

"What has become of their descendants—of those portraits?"

"They became extinct thousands of years ago."

She became silent again, lost in reverie. The agitation of my mind was not longer endurable. I was too near the acme of curiosity to longer delay. I threw reserve aside and not without fear and trembling faltered out:

"Where are the men of this country? Where do they stay?"

"There are none," was the startling reply. "*The race became extinct three thousand years ago.*"

CHAPTER II.

I trembled at the suggestion of my own thoughts. Was this an enchanted country? Where the lovely blonde women fairies—or some weird beings of different specie, human only in form? Or was I dreaming?

"I do not believe I understand you," I said. "I never heard of a country where there were no men. In my land they are so very, very important."

"Possibly," was the placid answer.

"And you are really a nation of women?"

"Yes," she said. "And have been for the last three thousand years."

"Will you tell me how this wonderful change came about?"

"Certainly. But in order to do it, I must go back to our very remote ancestry. The civilization that I shall begin with must have resembled the present condition of your own country as you describe it. Prisons and punishments were prevalent throughout the land."

I inquired how long prisons and places of punishment had been abolished in Mizora.

"For more than two thousand years," she replied. "I have no personal knowledge of crime. When I speak of it, it is wholly from an historical standpoint. A theft has not been committed in this country for many many centuries. And those minor crimes, such as envy, jealousy, malice and falsehood, disappeared a long time ago. You will not find a citizen in Mizora who possesses the slightest trace of any of them."

"Did they exist in earlier times?"

"Yes. Our oldest histories are but records of a succession of dramas in which the actors were continually striving for power and exercising all of those ancient qualities of mind to obtain it. Plots, intrigues, murders and wars, were the active employments of the very ancient rulers of our land. As soon as death laid its inactivity upon one actor, another took his place. It might have continued so; and we might still be repeating the old tragedy but for one singular event. In the history of your own people you have no doubt observed that the very thing plotted, intrigued and labored for, has in accomplishment proved the ruin of its projectors. You will remark this in the history I am about to relate.

"Main ages ago this country was peopled by two races—male and female. The male race were rulers in public and domestic life. Their supremacy had come down from pre-historic time, when strength of muscle was the only master. Woman was a beast of burden. She was regarded as inferior to man, mentally as well as physically. This idea prevailed through centuries of the earlier civilization, even after enlightenment had brought to her a chivalrous regard from men. But this regard was bestowed only upon the women of their own household, by the rich and powerful. Those women who had not been fortunate enough to have been born in such a sphere of life toiled early and late, in sorrow and privation, for a mere pittance that was barely sufficient to keep the flame of life from going out. Their labor was more arduous than men's, and their wages lighter.

"The government consisted of an aristocracy, a fortunate few, who were continually at strife with one another to gain supremacy of power, or an acquisition of territory. Wars, famine and pestilence were of frequent occurrence. Of the subjects, male and female, some had everything to render life a pleasure, while others had nothing. Poverty, oppression and wretchedness was the lot of the many. Power, wealth and luxury the dower of the few.

"Children came into the world undesired even by those who were able to rear them, and often after an attempt had been made to prevent their coming alive. Consequently numbers of them were deformed, not only physically, but mentally. Under these conditions life was a misery to the larger part of the human race, and to end it by self-destruction was taught by their religion to be a crime punishable with eternal torment by quenchless fire.

"But a revolution was at hand. Stinted toil rose up, armed and wrathful, against opulent oppression. The struggle was long and tragical, and was waged with such rancor and desperate persistence by the insurrectionists, that their women and children began to supply the places vacated by fallen fathers, husbands and brothers. It ended in victory for them. They demanded a form of government that should be the property of all. It was granted, limiting its privileges to adult male citizens.

"The first representative government lasted a century. In that time civilization had taken an advance far excelling the progress made in three centuries previous. So surely does the mind crave freedom for its perfect development. The consciousness of liberty is an ennobling element in human nature. No nation can become universally moral until it is absolutely FREE.

"But this first Republic had been diseased from its birth. Slavery had existed in certain districts of the nation. It was really the remains of a former and more degraded state of society which the new government, in the exultation of its own triumphant inauguration, neglected or lacked the wisdom to remedy. A portion of the country refused to admit slavery within its territory, but pledged itself not to interfere with that which had. Enmities, however, arose between the two sections, which, after years of repression and useless conciliation, culminated in another civil war. Slavery had resolved to absorb more territory, and the free territory had resolved that it should not. The war that followed in consequence severed forever the fetters of the slave and was the primary cause of the extinction of the male race.

"The inevitable effect of slavery is enervating and demoralizing. It is a canker that eats into the vitals of any nation that harbors it, no matter what form it assumes. The free territory had all the vigor, wealth and capacity for long endurance that self-dependence gives. It was in every respect prepared for a long and severe struggle. Its forces were collected in the name of the united government.

"Considering the marked inequality of the combatants the war would necessarily have been of short duration. But political corruption had crept into the trust places of the government, and unscrupulous politicians and office-seekers saw too many opportunities to harvest wealth from a continuation of the war. It was to their interest to prolong it, and they did. They placed in the most responsible positions of the army, military men whose incapacity was well known to them, and sustained them there while the country wept its maimed and dying sons.

"The slave territory brought to the front its most capable talent. It would have conquered had not the resources against which it contended been almost unlimited. Utterly worn out, every available means of supply being exhausted, it collapsed from internal weakness.

"The general government, in order to satisfy the clamors of the distressed and impatient people whose sons were being sacrificed, and whose taxes were increasing, to prolong the war had kept removing and reinstating military commanders, but always of reliable incapacity.

"A man of mediocre intellect and boundless self-conceit happened to be the commander-in-chief of the government army when the insurrection collapsed. The politicians, whose nefarious scheming had prolonged the war, saw their opportunity for furthering their own interests by securing his popularity. They assumed him to be the greatest military genius that the world had ever produced; as evidenced by his success where so many others had failed. It was known that he had never risked a battle until he was assured that his own soldiers were better equipped and outnumbered the enemy. But the politicians asserted that such a precaution alone should mark him as an extraordinary military genius. The deluded people accepted him as a hero.

"The politicians exhausted their ingenuity in inventing honors for him. A new office of special military eminence, with a large salary attached, was created for him. He was burdened with distinctions and emoluments, always worked by the politicians, for their benefit. The nation, following the lead of the political leaders, joined in their adulation. It failed to perceive the dangerous path that leads to anarchy and despotism—the worship of one man. It had unfortunately selected one who was cautious and undemonstrative, and who had become convinced that he really was the greatest prodigy that the world had ever produced.

"He was made President, and then the egotism and narrow selfishness of the man began to exhibit itself. He assumed all the prerogatives of royalty that his position would permit. He elevated his obscure and numerous relatives to responsible offices. Large salaries were paid them and intelligent clerks hired by the Government to perform their official duties.

"Corruption spread into every department, but the nation was blind to its danger. The few who did perceive the weakness and presumption of the hero were silenced by popular opinion.

"A second term of office was given him, and then the real character of the man began to display itself before the people. The whole nature of the man was selfish and stubborn. The strongest mental trait possessed by him was cunning.

"His long lease of power and the adulation of his political beneficiaries, acting upon a superlative self-conceit, imbued him with the belief that he had really rendered his country a service so inestimable that it would be impossible for it to entirely liquidate it. He exalted to unsuitable public offices his most intimate friends. They grew suddenly exclusive and aristocratic, forming marriages with eminent families.

"He traveled about the country with his entire family, at the expense of the Government, to gradually prepare the people for the ostentation of royalty. The cities and towns that he visited furnished fetes, illuminations, parades and every variety of entertainment that could be thought of or invented for his amusement or glorification. Lest the parade might not be sufficiently gorgeous or demonstrative he secretly sent agents to prepare the programme and size of his reception, always at the expense of the city he intended to honor with his presence.

"He manifested a strong desire to subvert the will of the people to his will. When informed that a measure he had proposed was unconstitutional, he requested that the constitution be changed. His intimate friends he placed in the most important and trustworthy positions under the Government, and protected them with the power of his own office.

"Many things that were distasteful and unlawful in a free government were flagrantly flaunted in the face of the people, and were followed by other slow, but sure, approaches to the usurpation of the liberties of the Nation. He urged the Government to double his salary as President, and it complied.

"There had long existed a class of politicians who secretly desired to convert the Republic into an Empire, that they might secure greater power and opulence. They had seen in the deluded enthusiasm of the people for one man, the opportunity for which they had long waited and schemed. He was unscrupulous and ambitious, and power had become a necessity to feed the cravings of his vanity.

"The Constitution of the country forbade the office of President to be occupied by one man for more than two terms. The Empire party proposed to amend it, permitting the people to elect a President for any number of terms, or for life if they choose. They tried to persuade the people that the country owed the greatest General of all time so distinctive an honor. They even claimed that it was necessary to the preservation of the Government; that his popularity could command an army to sustain him if he called for it.

"But the people had begun to penetrate the designs of the hero, and bitterly denounced his resolution to seek a third term of power. The terrible corruptions that had been openly protected by him, had advertised him as criminally unfit for so responsible an office. But, alas! the people had delayed too long. They had taken a young elephant into the palace. They had petted and fed him and admired his bulky growth, and now they could not remove him without destroying the building.

"The politicians who had managed the Government so long, proved that they had more power than the people They succeeded, by practices that were common with politicians in those days, in getting him nominated for a third term. The people, now thoroughly alarmed, began to see their past folly and delusion. They made energetic efforts to defeat his election. But they were unavailing. The politicians had arranged the ballot, and when the counts were published, the hero was declared President for life. When too late the deluded people discovered that they had helped dig the grave for the corpse of their civil liberty, and those who were loyal and had been misled saw it buried with unavailing regret. The undeserved popularity bestowed upon a narrow and selfish nature had been its ruin. In his inaugural address he declared that nothing but the will of the people governed him. He had not desired the office; public life was distasteful to him, yet he was willing to sacrifice himself for the good of his country.

"Had the people been less enlightened, they might have yielded without a murmur; but they had enjoyed too long the privileges of a free Government to see it usurped without a struggle. Tumult and disorder prevailed over the country. Soldiers were called out to protect the new Government, but numbers of them refused to obey. The consequence was they fought among themselves. A dissolution of the Government was the result. The General they had lauded so greatly failed to bring order out of chaos; and the schemers who had foisted him into power, now turned upon him with the fury of treacherous natures when foiled of their prey. Innumerable factions sprung up all over the land, each with a leader ambitious and hopeful of subduing the whole to his rule. They fought until the extermination of the race became imminent, when a new and unsuspected power arose and mastered.

"The female portion of the nation had never had a share in the Government. Their privileges were only what the chivalry or kindness of the men permitted. In law, their rights were greatly inferior. The evils of anarchy fell with direct effect upon them. At first, they organized for mutual protection from the lawlessness that prevailed. The organizations grew, united and developed into military power. They used their power wisely, discreetly, and effectively. With consummate skill and energy they gathered the reins of Government in their own hands.

"Their first aim had been only to force the country into peace. The anarchy that reigned had demoralized society, and they had suffered most. They had long pleaded for an equality of citizenship with men, but had pleaded in vain. They now remembered it, and resolved to keep the Government that their wisdom and power had restored. They had been hampered in educational progress. Colleges and all avenues to higher intellectual development had been rigorously closed against them. The professional pursuits of life were denied them. But a few, with sublime courage and energy, had forced their way into them amid the revilings of some of their own sex and opposition of the men. It was these brave spirits who had earned their liberal cultivation with so much difficulty, that had organized and directed the new power. They generously offered to form a Government that should be the property of all intelligent adult citizens, not criminal.

"But these wise women were a small minority. The majority were ruled by the remembrance of past injustice. *They* were now the power, and declared their intention to hold the Government for a century.

"They formed a Republic, in which they remedied many of the defects that had marred the Republic of men. They constituted the Nation an integer which could never be disintegrated by States' Rights ideas or the assumption of State sovereignty.

"They proposed a code of laws for the home government of the States, which every State in the Union ratified as their State Constitution, thus making a uniformity and strength that the Republic of men had never known or suspected attainable.

"They made it a law of every State that criminals could be arrested in any State they might flee to, without legal authority, other than that obtained in the vicinity of the crime. They made a law that criminals, tried and convicted of crime, could not be pardoned without the sanction of seventy-five out of one hundred educated and disinterested people, who should weigh the testimony and render their decision under oath. It is scarcely necessary to add that few criminals ever were pardoned. It removed from the office of Governor the responsibility of pardoning, or rejecting pardons as a purely personal privilege. It abolished the power of rich criminals to bribe their escape from justice; a practice that had secretly existed in the former Republic.

"In forming their Government, the women, who were its founders, profited largely by the mistakes or wisdom displayed in the Government of men. Neither the General Government, nor the State Government, could be independent of the other. A law of the Union could not become such until ratified by every State Legislature. A State law could not become constitutional until ratified by Congress.

"In forming the State Constitutions, laws were selected from the different State Constitutions that had proven wise for State Government during the former Republic. In the Republic of men, each State had made and ratified its own laws, independent of the General Government. The consequence was, no two States possessed similar laws.

"To secure strength and avoid confusion was the aim of the founders of the new Government. The Constitution of the National Government provided for the exclusion of the male sex from all affairs and privileges for a period of one hundred years.

"At the end of that time not a representative of the sex was in existence."

CHAPTER III.

I expressed my astonishment at her revelation. Their social life existed under conditions that were incredible to me. Would it be an impertinence to ask for an explanation that I might comprehend? Or was it really the one secret they possessed and guarded from discovery, a mystery that must forever surround them with a halo of doubt, the suggestion of uncanny power? I spoke as deprecatingly as I could. The Preceptress turned upon me a calm but penetrating gaze.

"Have we impressed you as a mysterious people?" she asked.

"Very, very much!" I exclaimed. "I have at times been oppressed by it."

"You never mentioned it," she said, kindly.

"I could not find an opportunity to," I said.

"It is the custom in Mizora, as you have no doubt observed, never to make domestic affairs a topic of conversation outside of the family, the only ones who would be interested in them; and this refinement has kept you from the solution of our social system. I have no hesitancy in gratifying your wish to comprehend it. The best way to do it is to let history lead up to it, if you have the patience to listen."

I assured her that I was anxious to hear all she chose to tell. She then resumed:

"The prosperity of the country rapidly increased under the rule of the female Presidents. The majority of them were in favor of a high state of morality, and they enforced it by law and practice. The arts and sciences were liberally encouraged and made rapid advancement. Colleges and schools flourished vigorously, and every branch of education was now open to women.

"During the Republic of men, the government had founded and sustained a military and naval academy, where a limited number of the youth of the country were educated at government expense. The female government re-organized the institutions, substituting the youth of their own sex. They also founded an academy of science, which was supplied with every facility for investigation and progress. None but those having a marked predilection for scientific research could obtain admission, and then it was accorded to demonstrated ability only. This drew to the college the best female talent in the country. The number of applicants was not limited.

"Science had hitherto been, save by a *very* few, an untrodden field to women, but the encouragement and rare facilities offered soon revealed latent talent that developed rapidly. Scarcely half a century had elapsed before the pupils of the college had effected by their discoveries some remarkable changes in living, especially in the prevention and cure of diseases.

"However prosperous they might become, they could not dwell in political security with a portion of the citizens disfranchised. The men were resolved to secure their former power. Intrigues and plots against the government were constantly in force among them. In order to avert another civil war, it was finally decided to amend the constitution, and give them an equal share in the ballot. They had no sooner obtained that than the old practices of the former Republic were resorted to to secure their supremacy in government affairs. The women looked forward to their former subjugation as only a matter of time, and bitterly regretted their inability to prevent it. But at the crisis, a prominent scientist proposed to let the race die out. Science had revealed the Secret of Life."

She ceased speaking, as though I fully understood her.

"I am more bewildered than ever," I exclaimed. "I cannot comprehend you."

"Come with me," she said.

I followed her into the Chemist's Laboratory. She bade me look into a microscope that she designated, and tell her what I saw.

"An exquisitely minute cell in violent motion," I answered.

"Daughter," she said, solemnly, "you are now looking upon the germ of *all* Life, be it animal or vegetable, a flower or a human being, it has that one common beginning. We have advanced far enough in Science to control its development. Know that the MOTHER is the only important part of all life. In the lowest organisms no other sex is apparent."

I sat down and looked at my companion in a frame of mind not easily described. There was an intellectual grandeur in her look and mien that was impressive. Truth sat, like a coronet, upon her brow. The revelation I had so longed for, I now almost regretted. It separated me so far from these beautiful, companionable beings.

"Science has instructed you how to supercede Nature," I said, finally.

"By no means. It has only taught us how to make her obey us. We cannot *create* Life. We cannot develop it. But we can control Nature's processes of development as we will. Can you deprecate such a power? Would not your own land be happier without idiots, without lunatics, without deformity and disease?"

"You will give me little hope of any radical change in my own lifetime when I inform you that deformity, if extraordinary, becomes a source of revenue to its possessor."

"All reforms are of slow growth," she said. "The moral life is the highest development of Nature. It is evolved by the same slow processes, and like the lower life, its succeeding forms are always higher ones. Its ultimate perfection will be mind, where all happiness shall dwell, where pleasure shall find fruition, and desire its ecstasy.

"It is the duty of every generation to prepare the way for a higher development of the next, as we see demonstrated by Nature in the fossilized remains of long extinct animal life, a preparatory condition for a higher form in the next evolution. If you do not enjoy the fruit of your labor in your own lifetime, the generation that follows you will be the happier for it. Be not so selfish as to think only of your own narrow span of life."

"By what means have you reached so grand a development?" I asked.

"By the careful study of, and adherence to, Nature's laws. It was long years—I should say centuries—before the influence of the coarser nature of men was eliminated from the present race.

"We devote the most careful attention to the Mothers of our race. No retarding mental or moral influences are ever permitted to reach her. On the contrary, the most agreeable contacts with nature, all that can cheer and ennoble in art or music surround her. She is an object of interest and tenderness to all who meet her. Guarded from unwholesome agitation, furnished with nourishing and proper diet—both mental and physical—the child of a Mizora mother is always an improvement upon herself. With us, childhood has no sorrows. We believe, and the present condition of our race proves, that a being environed from its birth with none but elevating influences, will grow up amiable and intelligent though inheriting unfavorable tendencies.

"On this principle we have ennobled our race and discovered the means of prolonging life and youthful loveliness far beyond the limits known by our ancestors.

"Temptation and necessity will often degrade a nature naturally inclined and desirous to be noble. We early recognized this fact, and that a nature once debased by crime would transmit it to posterity. For this reason we never permitted a convict to have posterity."

"But how have you become so beautiful?" I asked. "For, in all my journeys, I have not met an uncomely face or form. On the contrary, all the Mizora women have perfect bodies and lovely features."

"We follow the gentle guidance of our mother, Nature. Good air and judicious exercise for generations and generations before us have helped. Our ancestors knew the influence of art, sculpture, painting and music, which they were trained to appreciate."

"But has not nature been a little generous to you?" I inquired.

"Not more so than she will be to any people who follow her laws. When you first came here you had an idea that you could improve nature by crowding your lungs and digestive organs into a smaller space than she, the maker of them, intended them to occupy.

"If you construct an engine, and then cram it into a box so narrow and tight that it cannot move, and then crowd on the motive power, what would you expect?

"Beautiful as you think my people, and as they really are, yet, by disregarding nature's laws, or trying to thwart her intentions, in a few generations to come, perhaps even in the next, we could have coarse features and complexions, stoop shoulders and deformity.

"It has required patience, observation and care on the part of our ancestors to secure to us the priceless heritage of health and perfect bodies. Your people can acquire them by the same means."

CHAPTER IV.

As to Physical causes, I am inclined to doubt altogether of their
operation in this particular; nor do I think that men owe anything
of their temper or genius to the air, food, or climate.—*Bacon.*

I listened with the keenest interest to this curious and instructive history; and
when the Preceptress had ceased speaking. I expressed my gratitude for her kindness.
There were many things about which I desired information, but particularly their
method of eradicating disease and crime. These two evils were the prominent
afflictions of all the civilized nations I knew. I believed that I could comprehend
enough of their method of extirpation to benefit my own country. Would she kindly
give it?

"I shall take Disease first," she said, "as it is a near relative of Crime. You look
surprised. You have known life-long and incurable invalids who were not criminals.
But go to the squalid portion of any of your large cities, where Poverty and Disease go
hand in hand, where the child receives its life and its first nourishment from a haggard
and discontented mother. Starvation is her daily dread. The little tendernesses that
make home the haven of the heart, are never known to her. Ill-fed, ill-clothed, ill-
cherished, all that *might* be refined and elevated in her nature, if properly cultivated, is
choked into starveling shapes by her enemy—Want.

"If you have any knowledge of nature, ask yourself if such a condition of birth
and infancy is likely to produce a noble, healthy human being? Do your agriculturists
expect a stunted, neglected tree to produce rare and luscious fruit?"

I was surprised at the Preceptress' graphic description of wretchedness, so familiar
to all the civilized nations that I knew, and asked:

"Did such a state of society ever exist in this country?"

"Ages ago it was as marked a social condition of this land as it is of your own to-
day. The first great move toward eradicating disease was in providing clean and
wholesome food for the masses. It required the utmost rigor of the law to destroy the
pernicious practice of adulteration. The next endeavor was to crowd poverty out of the
land. In order to do this the Labor question came first under discussion, and resulted
in the establishment in every state of a Board of Arbitration that fixed the price of
labor on a per cent, of the profits of the business. Public and private charities were
forbidden by law as having an immoral influence upon society. Charitable institutions
had long been numerous and fashionable, and many persons engaged in them as
much for their own benefit as that of the poor. It was not always the honest and
benevolent ones who became treasurers, nor were the funds always distributed among
the needy and destitute, or those whom they were collected for. The law put a stop to

the possibility of such frauds, and of professional impostors seeking alms. Those who needed assistance were supplied with work—respectable, independent work—furnished by the city or town in which they resided. A love of industry, its dignity and independence, was carefully instilled into every young mind. There is no country but what ought to provide for everyone of its citizens a comfortable, if not luxurious, home by humane legislation on the labor question.

"The penitentiaries were reconstructed by the female government. One half the time formerly allotted to labor was employed in compulsory education. Industrial schools were established in every State, where all the mechanical employments were taught free. Objects of charity were sent there and compelled to become self supporting. These industrial schools finally became State Colleges, where are taught, free, all the known branches of knowledge, intellectual and mechanical.

"Pauperism disappeared before the wide reaching influence of these industrial schools, but universal affluence had not come. It could not exist until education had become universal.

"With this object in view, the Government forbade the employment of any citizen under the age of twenty-one, and compelled their attendance at school up to that time. At the same time a law was passed that authorized the furnishing of all school-room necessaries out of the public funds. If a higher education were desired the State Colleges furnished it free of all expenses contingent.

"All of these measures had a marked influence in improving the condition of society, but not all that was required. The necessity for strict sanitary laws became obvious. Cities and towns and even farms were visited, and everything that could breed malaria, or produce impure air, was compelled to be removed. Personal and household cleanliness at last became an object of public interest, and inspectors were appointed who visited families and reported the condition of their homes. All kinds of out-door sports and athletic exercises were encouraged and became fashionable.

"All of these things combined, made a great improvement in the health and vigor of our race, but still hereditary diseases lingered.

"There were many so enfeebled by hereditary disease they had not enough energy to seek recuperation, and died, leaving offspring as wretched, who in turn followed their parents' example.

"Statistics were compiled, and physician's reports circulated, until a law was passed prohibiting the perpetuity of diseased offspring. But, although disease became less prevalent, it did not entirely disappear. The law could only reach the most deplorable afflictions, and was eventually repealed.

"As the science of therapeutics advanced, all diseases—whether hereditary or acquired—were found to be associated with abnormal conditions of the blood. A microscopic examination of a drop of blood enabled the scientist to determine the character and intensity of any disease, and at last to effect its elimination from the system.

"The blood is the primal element of the body. It feeds the flesh, the nerves, the muscles, the brain. Disease cannot exist when it is in a natural condition. Countless experiments have determined the exact properties of healthy blood and how to produce it. By the use of this knowledge we have eliminated hereditary diseases, and developed into a healthy and moral people. For people universally healthy is sure of being moral. Necessity begets crime. It is the *wants* of the ignorant and debased that suggests theft. It is a diseased fancy, or a mind ignorant of the laws that govern the development of human nature, that could attribute to offspring hated before birth: infancy and childhood neglected; starved, ill-used in every way, a disposition and character, amiable and humane and likely to become worthy members of society. The reverse is almost inevitable. Human nature relapses into the lower and baser instincts of its earlier existence, when neglected, ill-used and *ignorant*. All of those lovely traits of character which excite the enthusiast, such as gratitude, honor, charity are the results of education only. They are not the natural instincts of the human mind, but the cultivated ones.

"The most rigid laws were passed in regard to the practice of medicine. No physician could become a practitioner until examined and authorized to do so by the State Medical College. In order to prevent favoritism, or the furnishing of diplomas to incompetent applicants, enormous penalties were incurred by any who would sign such. The profession long ago became extinct. Every mother is a family physician. That is, she obeys the laws of nature in regard to herself and her children, and they never need a doctor.

"Having become healthy and independent of charity, crime began to decrease naturally. The conditions that had bred and fostered petty crimes having ceased to exist, the natures that had inherited them rose above their influence in a few generations, and left honorable posterity.

"But crime in its grossest form is an ineradicable hereditary taint. Generation after generation may rise and disappear in a family once tainted with it, without displaying it, and then in a most unexpected manner it will spring up in some descendant, violent and unconquerable.

"We tried to eliminate it as we had disease, but failed. It was an inherited molecular structure of the brain. Science could not reconstruct it. The only remedy was annihilation. Criminals had no posterity."

"I am surprised," I interrupted, "that possessing the power to control the development of the body, you should not do so with the mind."

"If we could we would produce genius that could discover the source of all life. We can control Cause and Effect, but we cannot create Cause. We do not even know its origin. What the perfume is to the flower, the intellect is to the body; a secret that

Nature keeps to herself. For a thousand years our greatest minds have sought to discover its source, and we are as far from it to-day as we were a thousand years ago."

"How then have you obtained your mental superiority?" I inquired.

"By securing to our offspring perfect, physical and mental health. Science has taught us how to evolve intellect by following demonstrated laws. I put a seed into the ground and it comes up a little green slip, that eventually becomes a tree. When I planted the seed in congenial soil, and watered and tended the slip, I assisted Nature. But I did not create the seed nor supply the force that made it develop into a tree, nor can I define that force."

"What has produced the exquisite refinement of your people?"

"Like everything else, it is the result of gradual development aiming at higher improvement. By following strictly the laws that govern the evolution of life, we control the formation of the body and brain. Strong mental traits become intensified by cultivation from generation to generation and finally culminate in one glorious outburst of power, called Genius. But there is one peculiarity about mind. It resembles that wonderful century plant which, after decades of developing, flowers and dies. Genius is the long unfolding bloom of mind, and leaves no posterity. We carefully prepare for the future development of Genius. We know that our children will be neither deformed nor imbecile, but we watch the unfolding of their intellects with the interest of a new revelation. We guide them with the greatest care.

"I could take a child of your people with inherited weakness of body and mind. I should rear it on proper food and exercise—both mental and physical—and it would have, when matured, a marked superiority to its parents. It is not what Nature has done for us, it is what we have done for her, that makes us a race of superior people."

"The qualities of mind that are the general feature of your people," I remarked, "are so very high, higher than our estimate of Genius. How was it arrived at?"

"By the processes I have just explained. Genius is always a leader. A genius with us has a subtlety of thought and perception beyond your power of appreciation. All organized social bodies move intellectually in a mass, with their leader just ahead of them."

"I have visited, as a guest, a number of your families, and found their homes adorned with paintings and sculpture that would excite wondering admiration in my own land as rare works of art, but here they are only the expression of family taste and culture. Is that a quality of intellect that has been evolved, or is it a natural endowment of your race?"

"It is not an endowment, but has been arrived at by the same process of careful cultivation. Do you see in those ancient portraits a variety of striking colors? There is not a suggestion of harmony in any of them. On the contrary, they all display violent contrasts of color. The originals of them trod this land thousands of years ago. Many of the colors, we know, were unknown to them. Color is a faculty of the mind that is wholly the result of culture. In the early ages of society, it was known only in the coarsest and most brilliant hues. A conception and appreciation of delicate harmonies in color is evidence of a superior and refined mentality. If you will notice it, the illiterate of your own land have no taste for or idea of the harmony of color. It is the same with sound. The higher we rise in culture, the more difficult we are to please in music. Our taste becomes critical."

I had been revolving some things in my mind while the Preceptress was speaking, and I now ventured to express them. I said:

"You tell me that generations will come and go before a marked change can occur in a people. What good then would it do me or mine to study and labor and investigate in or to teach my people how to improve? They can not comprehend progress. They have not learned by contact, as I have in Mizora, how to appreciate it. I should only waste life and happiness in trying to persuade them to get out of the ruts they have traveled so long; they think there are no other roads. I should be reviled, and perhaps persecuted. My doctrines would be called visionary and impracticable. I think I had better use my knowledge for my own kindred, and let the rest of the world find out the best way it can."

The Preceptress looked at me with mild severity. I never before had seen so near an approach to rebuke in her grand eyes.

"What a barbarous, barbarous idea!" she exclaimed. "Your country will never rise above its ignorance and degradation, until out of its mental agony shall be evolved a nature kindled with an ambition that burns for Humanity instead of self. It will be the nucleus round which will gather the timid but anxious, and *then* will be lighted that fire which no waters can quench. It burns for the liberty of thought. Let human nature once feel the warmth of its beacon fires, and it will march onward, defying all obstacles, braving all perils till it be won. Human nature is ever reaching for the unattained. It is that little spark within us that has an undying life. When we can no longer use it, it flies elsewhere."

CHAPTER V.

I had long contemplated a trip to the extreme southern boundary of Mizora. I had often inquired about it, and had always been answered that it was defined by an impassable ocean. I had asked them to describe it to me, for the Mizora people have a happy faculty of employing tersely expressive language when necessary; but I was always met with the surprising answer that no tongue in Mizora was eloquent enough to portray the wonders that bounded Mizora on the south. So I requested the Preceptress to permit Wauna to accompany me as a guide and companion; a request she readily complied with.

"Will you be afraid or uneasy about trusting her on so long a journey with no companion or protector but me?" I asked.

The Preceptress smiled at my question.

"Why should I be afraid, when in all the length and breadth of our land there is no evil to befall her, or you either. Strangers are friends in Mizora, in one sense of the word, when they meet. You will both travel as though among time endeared associates. You will receive every attention, courtesy and kindness that would be bestowed upon near and intimate acquaintances. No, in this land, mothers do not fear to send their daughters alone and unrecommended among strangers."

When speed was required, the people of Mizora traveled altogether by air ships. But when the pleasure of landscape viewing, and the delight and exhilaration of easy progress is desired, they use either railroad cars or carriages.

Wauna and I selected an easy and commodious carriage. It was propelled by compressed air, which Wauna said could be obtained whenever we needed a new supply at any village or country seat.

Throughout the length and breadth of Mizora the roads were artificially made. Cities, towns, and villages were provided with paved streets, which the public authorities kept in a condition of perfect cleanliness. The absence of all kinds of animals rendered this comparatively easy. In alluding to this once in the presence of the Preceptress, she startled me by the request that I should suggest to my people the advantage to be derived from substituting machinery for animal labor.

"The association of animals is degrading," she asserted. "And you, who still live by tilling the soil, will find a marked change economically in dispensing with your beasts of burden. Fully four-fifths that you raise on your farms is required to feed your domestic animals. If your agriculture was devoted entirely to human food, it would make it more plentiful for the poor."

I did not like to tell her that I knew many wealthy people who housed and fed their domestic animals better than they did their tenants. She would have been disgusted with such a state of barbarism.

Country roads in Mizora were usually covered with a cement that was prepared from pulverized granite. They were very durable and very hard. Owing to their solidity, they were not as agreeable for driving as another kind of cement they manufactured. I have previously spoken of the peculiar style of wheel that was used on all kinds of light conveyances in Mizora, and rendered their progress over any road the very luxury of motion.

In our journey, Wauna took me to a number of factories, where the wonderful progress they had made in science continually surprised and delighted me. The spider and the silkworm had yielded their secret to these indefatigable searchers into nature's mysteries. They could spin a thread of gossamer, or of silk from their chemicals, of any width and length, and with a rapidity that was magical. Like everything else of that nature in Mizora, these discoveries had been purchased by the Government, and then made known to all.

They also manufactured ivory that I could not tell from the real article. I have previously spoken of their success in producing various kinds of marble and stone. A beautiful table that I saw made out of artificial ivory, had a painting upon the top of it. A deep border, composed of delicate, convoluted shells, extended round the top of the table and formed the shores of a mimic ocean, with coral reefs and tiny islands, and tangled sea-weeds and shining fishes sporting about in the pellucid water. The surface was of highly polished smoothness, and I was informed that the picture was *not* a painting but was formed of colored particles of ivory that had been worked in before the drying or solidifying process had been applied. In the same way they formed main beautiful combinations of marbles. The magnificent marble columns that supported the portico of my friend's house were all of artificial make. The delicate green leaves and creeping vines of ivy, rose, and eglantine, with their spray-like blossoms, were colored in the manufacturing process and chiseled out of the solid marble by the skillful hand of the artist.

It would be difficult for me to even enumerate all the beautiful arts and productions of arts that I saw in Mizora. Our journey was full of incidents of this kind.

Every city and town that we visited was like the introduction of a new picture. There was no sameness between any of them. Each had aimed at picturesqueness or stately magnificence, and neither had failed to obtain it. Looking back as I now do upon Mizora, it presents itself to me as a vast and almost limitless landscape, variegated with grand cities, lovely towns and villages, majestic hills and mountains crowned with glittering snows, or deep, delightful valleys veiled in scented vines.

Kindness, cordiality and courtesy met us on every side. It was at first quite novel for me to mingle among previously unheard-of people with such sociability, but I did as Wauna did, and I found it not only convenient but quite agreeable.

"I am the daughter of the Preceptress of the National College," said Wauna; and that was the way she introduced herself.

I noticed with what honor and high esteem the name of the Preceptress was regarded. As soon as it was known that the daughter of the Preceptress had arrived, the citizens of whatever city we had stopped in hastened to extend to her every courtesy and favor possible for them to bestow. She was the daughter of the woman who held the highest and most enviable position in the Nation. A position that only great intellect could secure in that country.

As we neared the goal of our journey, I noticed an increasing warmth of the atmosphere, and my ears were soon greeted with a deep, reverberating roar like continuous thunder. I have seen and heard Niagara, but a thousand Niagaras could not equal that deafening sound. The heat became oppressive. The light also from a cause of which I shall soon speak.

We ascended a promontory that jutted out from the main land a quarter of a mile, perhaps more. Wauna conducted me to the edge of the cliff and told me to look down. An ocean of whirlpools was before us. The maddened dashing and thundering of the mighty waters, and the awe they inspired no words can paint. Across such an abyss of terrors it was certain no vessel could sail. We took our glasses and scanned the opposite shore, which appeared to be a vast cataract as though the ocean was pouring over a precipice of rock. Wauna informed me that where the shore was visible it was a perpendicular wall of smooth rock.

Over head an arc of fire spanned the zenith from which depended curtains of rainbows waving and fluttering, folding and floating out again with a rapid and incessant motion. I asked Wauna why they had not crossed in air-ships, and she said they had tried it often but had always failed.

"In former times," she said, "when air-ships first came into use it was frequently attempted, but no voyager ever returned. We have long since abandoned the attempt, for now we know it to be impossible."

I looked again at that display of uncontrollable power. As I gazed it seemed to me I would be drawn down by the resistless fascination of terror. I grasped Wauna and she gently turned my face to the smiling landscape behind us. Hills and valleys, and sparkling cities veiled in foliage, with their numberless parks and fountains and statues sleeping in the soft light, gleaming lakes and wandering rivers that glittered and danced in the glorious atmosphere like prisoned sunbeams, greeted us like the alluring smile of love, and yet, for the first time since entering this lovely land, I felt myself a prisoner. Behind me was an impassable barrier. Before me, far beyond this gleaming vision of enchantment, lay another road whose privations and dangers I dreaded to attempt.

I felt as a bird might feel who has been brought from the free expanse of its wild forest-home, and placed in a golden cage where it drinks from a jeweled cup and eats daintier food than it could obtain in its own rude haunts. It pines for that precarious life; its very dangers and privations fill its breast with desire. I began to long with unutterable impatience to see once more the wild, rough scenes of my own nativity.

Memory began to recall them with softening touches. My heart yearned for my own; debased as compared with Mizora though they be, there was the congeniality of blood between us. I longed to see my own little one whose dimpled hands I had unclasped from my neck in that agonized parting. Whenever I saw a Mizora mother fondling her babe, my heart leapt with quick desire to once more hold my own in such loving embrace. The mothers of Mizora have a devotional love for their children. Their smiles and prattle and baby wishes are listened to with loving tenderness, and treated as matters of importance.

I was sitting beside a Mizora mother one evening, listening to some singing that I truly thought no earthly melody could surpass. I asked the lady if ever she had heard anything sweeter, and she answered, earnestly:

"Yes, the voices of my own children."

On our homeward journey, Wauna took me to a lake from the center of which we could see, with our glasses, a green island rising high above the water like an emerald in a silver setting.

"That," said Wauna, directing my attention to it, "is the last vestige of a prison left in Mizora. Would you like to visit it?"

I expressed an eager willingness to behold so curious a sight, and getting into a small pleasure boat, we started toward it. Boats are propelled in Mizora either by electricity or compressed air, and glide through the water with soundless swiftness.

As we neared the island I could perceive the mingling of natural and artificial attractions. We moored our boat at the foot of a flight of steps, hewn from the solid rock. On reaching the top, the scene spread out like a beautiful painting. Grottos, fountains, and cascades, winding walks and vine-covered bowers charmed us as we wandered about. In the center stood a medium-sized residence of white marble. We entered through a door opening on a wide piazza. Art and wealth and taste had adorned the interior with a generous hand. A library studded with books closely shut behind glass doors had a wide window that commanded an enchanting view of the lake, with its rippling waters sparkling and dimpling in the light. On one side of the mantelpiece hung a full length portrait of a lady, painted with startling naturalness.

"That," said Wauna, solemnly, "was the last prisoner in Mizora."

I looked with interested curiosity at a relic so curious in this land. It was a blonde woman with lighter colored eyes than is at all common in Mizora. Her long, blonde hair hung straight and unconfined over a dress of thick, white material. Her attitude and expression were dejected and sorrowful. I had visited prisons in my own land where red-handed murder sat smiling with indifference. I had read in newspapers, labored eloquence that described the stoicism of some hardened criminal as a trait of character to be admired. I had read descriptions where mistaken eloquence exerted itself to waken sympathy for a criminal who had never felt sympathy for his helpless and innocent victims, and I had felt nothing but creeping horror for it all. But gazing at this picture of undeniable repentance, tears of sympathy started to my eyes. Had she been guilty of taking a fellow-creature's life?

"Is she still living?" I asked by way of a preface.

"Oh, no, she has been dead for more than a century," answered Wauna.

"Was she confined here very long?"

"For life," was the reply.

"I should not believe," I said, "that a nature capable of so deep a repentance could be capable of so dark a crime as murder."

"Murder!" exclaimed Wauna in horror. "There has not been a murder committed in this land for three thousand years."

It was my turn to be astonished.

"Then tell me what dreadful crime she committed."

"She struck her child," said Wauna, sadly; "her little innocent, helpless child that Nature gave her to love and cherish, and make noble and useful and happy."

"Did she inflict a permanent injury?" I asked, with increased astonishment at this new phase of refinement in the Mizora character.

"No one can tell the amount of injury a blow does to a child. It may immediately show an obvious physical one; it may later develop a mental one. It may never seem to have injured it at all, and yet it may have shocked a sensitive nature and injured it permanently. Crime is evolved from perverted natures, and natures become perverted from ill-usage. It merges into a peculiar structure of the brain that becomes hereditary."

"What became of the prisoner's child?"

"It was adopted by a young lady who had just graduated at the State College of the State in which the mother resided. It was only five years old, and its mother's name was never mentioned to it or to anyone else. Long before that, the press had abolished the practice of giving any prominence to crime. That pernicious eloquence that in uncivilized ages had helped to nourish crime by a maudlin sympathy for the criminal, had ceased to exist. The young lady called the child daughter, and it called her mother."

"Did the real mother never want to see her child?"

"That is said to be a true picture of her," said Wauna; "and who can look at it and not see sorrow and remorse."

"How could you be so stern?" I asked, in wondering astonishment.

"Pity has nothing to do with crime," said Wauna, firmly. "You must look to humanity, and not to the sympathy one person excites when you are aiding enlightenment. That woman wandered about these beautiful grounds, or sat in this elegant home a lonely and unsympathized-with prisoner. She was furnished with books, magazines and papers, and every physical comfort. Sympathy for her lot was never offered her. Childhood is regarded by my people as the only period of life that is capable of knowing perfect happiness, and among us it is a crime greater than the heinousness of murder in your country, to deprive a human being of its childhood—in which cluster the only unalloyed sweets of life.

"A human being who remembers only pain, rebukes treatment in childhood, has lost the very flavor of existence, and the person who destroyed it is a criminal indeed."

CHAPTER VI.

There was one peculiarity about Mizora that I noticed soon after my arrival, but for various reasons have refrained from speaking of before now. It was the absence of houses devoted to religious worship.

In architecture Mizora displayed the highest perfection. Their colleges, art galleries, public libraries, opera houses, and all their public buildings were grand and beautiful. Never in any country, had I beheld such splendor in design and execution. Their superior skill in this respect, led me to believe that their temples of worship must be on a scale of magnificence beyond all my conceiving. I was eager to behold them. I looked often upon my first journeyings about their cities to discover them, but whenever I noticed an unusually imposing building, and asked what it was, it was always something else. I was frequently on the point of asking them to conduct me to some church that resembled my own in worship, (for I was brought up in strict compliance with the creeds, dogmas, and regulations of the Russo Greek Church) but I refrained, hoping that in time, I should be introduced to their religious ceremonies.

When time passed on, and no invitation was extended me, and I saw no house nor preparation for religious worship, nor even heard mention of any, I asked Wauna for an explanation. She appeared not to comprehend me, and I asked the question:

"Where do you perform your religious rites and ceremonies?"

She looked at me with surprise.

"You ask me such strange questions that sometimes I am tempted to believe you a relic of ancient mythology that has drifted down the centuries and landed on our civilized shores, or else have been gifted with a marvelous prolongation of life, and have emerged upon us from some cavern where you have lived, or slept for ages in unchanged possession of your ancient superstition."

"Have you, then," I asked in astonishment, "no religious temples devoted to worship?"

"Oh, yes, we have temples where we worship daily. Do you see that building?" nodding toward the majestic granite walls of the National College. "That is one of our most renowned temples, where the highest and the noblest in the land meet and mingle familiarly with the humblest in daily worship."

"I understand all that you wish to imply by that," I replied. "But have you no building devoted to divine worship; no temple that belongs specially to your Deity; to the Being that created you, and to whom you owe eternal gratitude and homage?"

"We have;" she answered grandly, with a majestic wave of her hand, and in that mellow, musical voice that was sweeter than the chanting of birds, she exclaimed:

"This vast cathedral, boundless as our wonder;
  Whose shining lamps yon brilliant mists[A] supply;

Its choir the winds, and waves; its organ thunder;
  Its dome the sky."

[Footnote A: Aurora Borealis]

"Do you worship Nature?" I asked.

"If we did, we should worship ourselves, for we are a part of Nature."

"But do you not recognize an invisible and incomprehensible Being that created you, and who will give your spirit an abode of eternal bliss, or consign it to eternal torments according as you have glorified and served him?"

"I am an atom of Nature;" said Wauna, gravely. "If you want me to answer your superstitious notions of religion, I will, in one sentence, explain, that the only religious idea in Mizora is: Nature is God, and God is Nature. She is the Great Mother who gathers the centuries in her arms, and rocks their children into eternal sleep upon her bosom."

"But how," I asked in bewildered astonishment, "how can you think of living without creeds, and confessionals? How can you prosper without prayer? How can you be upright, and honest, and true to yourselves and your friends without praying for divine grace and strength to sustain you? How can you be noble, and keep from envying your neighbors, without a prayer for divine grace to assist you to resist such temptation?"

"Oh, daughter of the dark ages," said Wauna, sadly, "turn to the benevolent and ever-willing Science. She is the goddess who has led us out of ignorance and superstition; out of degradation and disease, and every other wretchedness that superstitious, degraded humanity has known. She has lifted us above the low and the little, the narrow and mean in human thought and action, and has placed us in a broad, free, independent, noble, useful and grandly happy life."

"You have been favored by divine grace," I reiterated, "although you refuse to acknowledge it."

She smiled compassionately as she answered:

"She is the divinity who never turned a deaf ear to earnest and persistent effort in a sensible direction. But prayers to her must be *work*, resolute and conscientious *work*. She teaches that success in this world can only come to those who work for it. In your superstitious belief you pray for benefits you have never earned, possibly do not deserve, but expect to get simply because you pray for them. Science never betrays such partiality. The favors she bestows are conferred only upon the industrious."

"And you deny absolutely the efficacy of prayer?" I asked.

"If I could obtain anything by prayer alone, I would pray that my inventive faculty should be enlarged so that I might conceive and construct an air-ship that could cleave its way through that chaos of winds that is formed when two storms meet from opposite directions. It would rend to atoms one of our present make. But prayer will never produce an improved air-ship. We must dig into science for it. Our ancestors did not pray for us to become a race of symmetrically-shaped and universally healthy people, and expect that to effect a result. They went to work on scientific principles to root out disease and crime and want and wretchedness, and every degrading and retarding influence."

"Prayer never saved one of my ancestors from premature death," she continued, with a resolution that seemed determined to tear from my mind every fabric of faith in the consolations of divine interposition that had been a special part of my education, and had become rooted into my nature. "Disease, when it fastened upon the vitals of the young and beautiful and dearly-loved was stronger and more powerful than all the agonized prayers that could be poured from breaking hearts. But science, when solicited by careful study and experiment and investigation, offered the remedy. And *now*, we defy disease and have no fear of death until our natural time comes, and *then* it will be the welcome rest that the worn-out body meets with gratitude."

"But when you die," I exclaimed, "do you not believe you have an after life?"

"When I die," replied Wauna, "my body will return to the elements from whence it came. Thought will return to the force which gave it. The power of the brain is the one mystery that surrounds life. We know that the brain is a mechanical structure and acted upon by force; but how to analyze that force is still beyond our reach. You see that huge engine? We made it. It is a fine piece of mechanism. We know what it was made to do. We turn on the motive power, and it moves at the rate of a mile a minute if we desire it. Why should it move? Why might it not stand still? You say because of a law of nature that under the circumstances compels it to move. Our brain is like that engine—a wonderful piece of mechanism, and when the blood drives it, it displays the effects of force which we call Thought. We can see the engine move and we know what law of nature it obeys in moving. But the brain is a more mysterious structure, for the force which compels it to action we cannot analyze. The superstitious ancients called this mystery the soul."

"And do you discard that belief?" I asked, trembling and excited to hear such sacrilegious talk from youth so beautiful and pure.

"What our future is to be after dissolution no one knows," replied Wauna, with the greatest calmness and unconcern. "A thousand theories and systems of religion have risen and fallen in the history of the human family, and become the superstitions of the past. The elements that compose this body may construct the delicate beauty of a flower, or the green robe that covers the bosom of Mother Earth, but we cannot know."

"But that beautiful belief in a soul," I cried, in real anguish, "How can you discard it? How sever the hope that after death, we are again united to part no more? Those who have left us in the spring time of life, the bloom on their young cheeks suddenly paled by the cold touch of death, stand waiting to welcome us to an endless reunion."

"Alas, for your anguish, my friend," said Wauna, with pityng tenderness. "Centuries ago *my* people passed through that season of mental pain. That beautiful visionary idea of a soul must fade, as youth and beauty fade, never to return; for Nature nowhere teaches the existence of such a thing. It was a belief born of that agony of longing for happiness without alloy, which the children of earth in the long-ago ages hoped for, but never knew. Their lot was so barren of beauty and happiness, and the desire for it is, now and always has been, a strong trait of human character. The conditions of society in those earlier ages rendered it impossible to enjoy this life perfectly, and hope and longing pictured an imaginary one for an imaginary part of the body called the Soul. Progress and civilization have brought to us the ideal heaven of the ancients, and we receive from Nature no evidence of any other."

"But I do believe there is another," I declared. "And we ought to be prepared for it."

Wauna smiled. "What better preparation could you desire, then, than good works in this?" she asked.

"You should pray, and do penance for your sins," was my reply.

"Then," said Wauna, "we are doing the wisest penance every day. We are studying, investigating, experimenting in order that those who come after us may be happier than we. Every day Science is yielding us some new knowledge that will make living in the future still easier than now."

"I cannot conceive," I said, "how you are to be improved upon."

"When we manufacture fruit and vegetables from the elements, can you not perceive how much is to be gained? Old age and death will come later, and the labor of cultivation will be done away. Such an advantage will not be enjoyed during my lifetime. But we will labor to effect it for future generations."

"Your whole aim in life, then, is to work for the future of your race, instead of the eternal welfare of your own soul?" I questioned, in surprise.

"If Nature," said Wauna, "has provided us a future life, if that mysterious something that we call Thought is to be clothed in an etherealized body, and live in a world where decay is unknown, I have no fear of my reception there. Live *this* life usefully and nobly, and no matter if a prayer has never crossed your lips your happiness will be assured. A just and kind action will help you farther on the road to heaven than all the prayers that you can utter, and all the pains and sufferings that you can inflict upon the flesh, for it will be that much added to the happiness of this world. The grandest epitaph that could be written is engraved upon a tombstone in yonder cemetery. The subject was one of the pioneers of progress in a long-ago century, when progress fought its way with difficulty through ignorance and superstition. She suffered through life for the boldness of her opinions, and two centuries after, when they had become popular, a monument was erected to her memory, and has been preserved through thousands of years as a motto for humanity. The epitaph is simply this: 'The world is better for her having lived in it.'"

CHAPTER VII.

Not long after my conversation with Wauna, mentioned in the previous chapter, an event happened in Mizora of so singular and unexpected a character for that country that it requires a particular description. I refer to the death of a young girl, the daughter of the Professor of Natural History in the National College, whose impressive inaugural ceremonies I had witnessed with so much gratification. The girl was of a venturesome disposition, and, with a number of others, had gone out rowing. The boats they used in Mizora for that purpose were mere cockle shells. A sudden squall arose from which all could have escaped, but the reckless daring of this young girl cost her her life. Her boat was capsized, and despite the exertions made by her companions, she was drowned.

Her body was recovered before the news was conveyed to the mother. As the young companions surrounded it in the abandon of grief that tender and artless youth alone feels, had I not known that not a tie of consanguinity existed between them, I might have thought them a band of sisters mourning their broken number. It was a scene I never expect and sincerely hope never to witness again. It made the deeper impression upon me because I knew the expressions of grief were all genuine.

I asked Wauna if any of the dead girl's companions feared that her mother might censure them for not making sufficient effort to save her when her boat capsized. She looked at me with astonishment.

"Such a thought," she said, "will never occur to her nor to any one else in Mizora. I have not asked the particulars, but I know that everything was done that could have been done to save her. There must have been something extraordinarily unusual about the affair for all Mizora girls are expert swimmers, and there is not one but would put forth any exertion to save a companion."

I afterward learned that such had really been the case.

It developed upon the Preceptress to break the news to the afflicted mother. It was done in the seclusion of her own home. There was no manifestation of morbid curiosity among acquaintances, neighbors and friends. The Preceptress and one or two others of her nearest and most intimate friends called at the house during the first shock of her bereavement.

After permission had been given to view the remains, Wauna and I called at the house, but only entered the drawing-room. On a low cot, in an attitude of peaceful repose, lay the breathless sleeper. Her mother and sisters had performed for her the last sad offices of loving duty, and lovely indeed had they made the last view we should have of their dear one.

There was to be no ceremony at the house, and Wauna and I were in the cemetery when the procession entered. As we passed through the city, I noticed that every business house was closed. The whole city was sympathizing with sorrow. I never before saw so vast a concourse of people. The procession was very long and headed by the mother, dressed and veiled in black. Behind her were the sisters carrying the body. It rested upon a litter composed entirely of white rosebuds. The sisters wore white, their faces concealed by white veils. Each wore a white rosebud pinned upon her bosom. They were followed by a long procession of young girls, schoolmates and friends of the dead. They were all dressed in white, but were not veiled. Each one carried a white rosebud.

The sisters placed the litter upon rests at the side of the grave, and clasping hands with their mother, formed a semicircle about it. They were all so closely veiled that their features could not be seen, and no emotion was visible. The procession of young girls formed a circle inclosing the grave and the mourners, and began chanting a slow and sorrowful dirge. No words can paint the pathos and beauty of such a scene. My eye took in every detail that displayed that taste for the beautiful that compels the Mizora mind to mingle it with every incident of life. The melody sounded like a chorus of birds chanting, in perfect unison, a weird requiem over some dead companion.

DIRGE

She came like the Spring in its gladness
We received her with joy—we rejoiced in her promise
Sweet was her song as the bird's,
Her smile was as dew to the thirsty rose.
But the end came ere morning awakened,
While Dawn yet blushed in its bridal veil,
The leafy music of the woods was hushed in snowy shrouds.
Spring withered with the perfume in her hands;
A winter sleet has fallen upon the buds of June;
The ice-winds blow where yesterday zephyrs disported:
Life is not consummated
The rose has not blossomed, the fruit has perished in the flower,
The bird lies frozen under its mother's breast
Youth sleeps in round loveliness when age should lie withered and
  weary, and full of honor.
Then the grave would be welcome, and our tears would fall not.
The grave is not for the roses of youth;
We mourn the early departed.
Youth sleeps without dreams—
Without an awakening.

At the close of the chant, the mother first and then each sister took from her bosom the white rosebud and dropped it into the grave. Then followed her schoolmates and companions who each dropped in the bud she carried. A carpet of white rosebuds was thus formed, on which the body, still reclining upon its pillow of flowers, was gently lowered.

The body was dressed in white, and over all fell a veil of fine white tulle. A more beautiful sight I can never see than that young, lovely girl in her last sleep with the emblems of youth, purity and swift decay forming her pillow, and winding-sheet. Over this was placed a film of glass that rested upon the bottom and sides of the thin lining that covered the bottom and lower sides of the grave. The remainder of the procession of young girls then came forward and dropped their rosebuds upon it, completely hiding from view the young and beautiful dead.

The eldest sister then took a handful of dust and casting it into the grave, said in a voice broken, yet audible: "Mingle ashes with ashes, and dust with its original dust. To the earth whence it was taken, consign we the body of our sister." Each sister then threw in a handful of dust, and then with their mother entered their carriage, which immediately drove them home.

A beautiful silver spade was sticking in the soft earth that had been taken from the grave. The most intimate of the dead girls friends took a spadeful of earth and threw it into the open grave. Her example was followed by each one of the remaining companions until the grave was filled. Then clasping hands, they chanted a farewell to their departed companion and playmate. After which they strewed the grave with flowers until it looked like a bed of beauty, and departed.

I was profoundly impressed by the scene. Its solemnity, its beauty, and the universal expression of sorrow it had called forth. A whole city mourned the premature death of gifted and lovely youth. Alas! In my own unhappy country such an event would have elicited but a passing phrase of regret from all except the immediate family of the victim; for *there* sorrow is a guest at every heart, and leaves little room for sympathy with strangers.

The next day the mother was at her post in the National College; the daughters were at their studies, all seemingly calm and thoughtful, but showing no outward signs of grief excepting to the close observer. The mother was performing her accustomed duties with seeming cheerfulness, but now and then her mind would drop for a moment in sorrowful abstraction to be recalled with resolute effort and be fastened once more upon the necessary duty of life.

The sisters I often saw in those abstracted moods, and frequently saw them wiping away silent but unobtrusive tears. I asked Wauna for the meaning of such stoical reserve, and the explanation was as curious as were all the other things that I met with in Mizora.

"If you notice the custom of different grades of civilization in your own country," said Wauna, "you will observe that the lower the civilization the louder and more ostentatious is the mourning. True refinement is unobtrusive in everything, and while we do not desire to repress a natural and inevitable feeling of sorrow, we do desire to conceal and conquer it, for the reason that death is a law of nature that we cannot evade. And, although the death of a young person has not occurred in Mizora in the memory of any living before this, yet it is not without precedent. We are very prudent, but we cannot guard entirely against accident. It has cast a gloom over the whole city, yet we refrain from speaking of it, and strive to forget it because it cannot be helped."

"And can you see so young, so fair a creature perish without wanting to meet her again?"

"Whatever sorrow we feel," replied Wauna, solemnly, "we deeply realize how useless it is to repine. We place implicit faith in the revelations of Nature, and in no circumstances does she bid us expect a life beyond that of the body. That is a life of individual consciousness."

"How much more consoling is the belief of my people," I replied, triumphantly. "Their belief in a future reunion would sustain them through the sorrow of parting in this. It has been claimed that some have lived pure lives solely in the hope of meeting some one whom they loved, and who had died in youth and innocence."

Wauna smiled.

"You do not all have then the same fate in anticipation for your future life?" she asked.

"Oh, no!" I answered. "The good and the wicked are divided."

"Tell me some incident in your own land that you have witnessed, and which illustrates the religious belief of your country."

"The belief that we have in a future life has often furnished a theme for the poets of my own and other countries. And sometimes a quaint and pretty sentiment is introduced into poetry to express it."

"I should like to hear some such poetry. Can you recite any?"

"I remember an incident that gave birth to a poem that was much admired at the time, although I can recall but the two last stanzas of it. A rowing party, of which I was a member, once went out upon a lake to view the sunset. After we had returned to shore, and night had fallen upon the water in impenetrable darkness, it was discovered that one of the young men who had rowed out in a boat by himself was not with us. A storm was approaching, and we all knew that his safety lay in getting ashore before it broke. We lighted a fire, but the blaze could not be seen far in such inky darkness. We hallooed, but received no answer, and finally ceased our efforts. Then one of the young ladies who possessed a very high and clear soprano voice, began singing at the very top of her power. It reached the wanderer in the darkness, and he rowed straight toward it. From that time on he became infatuated with the singer, declaring that her voice had come to him in his despair like an angel's straight from heaven.

"She died in less than a year, and her last words to him were: 'Meet me in heaven.' He had always been recklessly inclined, but after that he became a model of rectitude and goodness. He wrote a poem that was dedicated to her memory. In it he described himself as a lone wanderer on a strange sea in the darkness of a gathering storm and no beacon to guide him, when suddenly he hears a voice singing which guides him safe to shore. He speaks of the beauty of the singer and how dear she became to him, but he still hears the song calling him across the ocean of death."

"Repeat what you remember of it," urged Wauna.

> "That face and form, have long since gone
>   Beyond where the day was lifted:
> But the beckoning song still lingers on,
>   An angels earthward drifted.
>
> And when death's waters, around me roar
>   And cares, like the birds, are winging:
> If I steer my bark to Heaven's shore
>   'Twill be by an angel's singing."

"Poor child of superstition," said Wauna, sadly. "Your belief has something pretty in it, but for your own welfare, and that of your people, you must get rid of it as we have got rid of the offspring of Lust. Our children come to us as welcome guests through portals of the holiest and purest affection. That love which you speak of, I know nothing about. I would not know. It is a degradation which mars your young life and embitters the memories of age. We have advanced beyond it. There is a cruelty in life," she added, compassionately, "which we must accept with stoicism as the inevitable. Justice to your posterity demands of you the highest and noblest effort of which your intellect is capable."

CHAPTER VIII.

The conversation that I had with Wauna gave me so much uneasiness that I sought her mother. I cannot express the shock I felt at hearing such youthful and innocent lips speak of the absurdity of religious forms, ceremonies, and creeds. She regarded my belief in them as a species of barbarism. But she had not convinced me. *I was resolved not to be convinced.* I believed she was in error.

Surely, I thought, a country so far advanced in civilization, and practicing such unexampled rectitude, must, according to my religious teaching, have been primarily actuated by religious principles which they had since abandoned. My only surprise was that they had not relapsed into immorality, after destroying church and creed, and I began to feel anxious to convince them of the danger I felt they were incurring in neglecting prayer and supplication at the throne to continue them in their progress toward perfection of mental and moral culture.

I explained my feelings to the Preceptress with great earnestness and anxiety for their future, intimating that I believed their immunity from disaster had been owing to Divine sufferance. "For no nation," I added, quoting from my memory of religious precepts, "can prosper without acknowledging the Christian religion."

She listened to me with great attention, and when I had finished, asked:

"How do you account for our long continuance in prosperity and progress, for it is more than a thousand years since we rooted out the last vestige of what you term religion, from the mind. We have had a long immunity from punishment. To what do you attribute it?"

I hesitated to explain what had been in my mind, but finally faltered out something about the absence of the male sex. I then had to explain that the prisons and penitentiaries of my own land, and of all other civilized lands that I knew of, were almost exclusively occupied by the male sex. Out of eight hundred penitentiary prisoners, not more than twenty or thirty would be women; and the majority of them could trace *their* crimes to man's infidelity.

"And what do you do to reform them?" inquired the Preceptress.

"We offer them the teachings of Christianity. All countries, however, differ widely in this respect. The government of my country is not as generous to prisoners as that of some others. In the United States every penitentiary is supplied with a minister who expounds the Gospel to the prisoners every Sunday; that is once every seven days."

"And what do they do the rest of the time?"

"They work."

"Are they ignorant?"

"Oh, yes, indeed;" I replied, earnestly. "You could not find one scholar in ten thousand of them. Their education is either very limited, or altogether deficient."

"Do the buildings they are confined in cost a great deal?"

"Vast sums of money are represented by them; and it often costs a community a great deal of money to send a criminal to the penitentiary. In some States the power to pardon rests entirely with the governor, and it frequently occurs that a desperate criminal, who has cost a county a great deal of money to get rid of him, will be pardoned by the governor, to please a relative, or, as it is sometimes believed, for a bribe."

"And do the people never think of educating their criminals instead of working them?

"That would be an expense to the government," I replied.

"If they would divide the time, and compel them to study half a day as rigorously as they make them work, it would soon make a vast change in their morals. Nothing so ennobles the mind as a broad and thorough education."

"They are all compelled to listen to religious instruction once a week," I answered. "That surely ought to make some improvement in them. I remember hearing an American lady relate her attendance at chapel service in a State penitentiary one Sunday. The minister's education was quite limited, as she could perceive from the ungrammatical language he used, but he preached sound orthodox doctrine. The text selected had a special application to his audience: 'Depart from me ye accursed, into everlasting torment prepared for the Devil and his angels.' There were eight hundred prisoners, and the minister assured them, in plain language, that such would surely be their sentence unless they repented."

"And that is what you call the consolations of religion, is it?" asked the Preceptress with an expression that rather disconcerted me; as though my zeal and earnestness entirely lacked the light of knowledge with which she viewed it.

"That is religious instruction;" I answered. "The minister exhorted the prisoners to pray and be purged of their sins. And it was good advice."

"But they might aver," persisted the Preceptress, "that they had prayed to be restrained from crime, and their prayers had not been answered."

"They didn't pray with enough faith, then;" I assured her in the confidence of my own belief. "That is wherein I think my own church is so superior to the other religions of the world," I added, proudly. "We can get the priest to absolve us from sin, and then we know we are rid of it, when he tells us so."

"But what assurance have you that the priest can do so?" asked the Preceptress.

"Because it is his duty to do so."

"Education will root out more sin than all your creeds can," gravely answered the Preceptress. "Educate your convicts and train them into controlling and subduing their criminal tendencies by *their own will*, and it will have more effect on their morals than all the prayers ever uttered. Educate them up to that point where they can perceive for themselves the happiness of moral lives, and then you may trust them to temptation without fear. The ideas you have expressed about dogmas, creeds and ceremonies are not new to us, though, as a nation, we do not make a study of them. They are very, very ancient. They go back to the first records of the traditionary history of man. And the farther you go back the deeper you plunge into ignorance and superstition.

"The more ignorant the human mind, the more abject was its slavery to religion. As history progresses toward a more diffuse education of the masses, the forms, ceremonies and beliefs in religion are continually changing to suit the advancement of intelligence; and when intelligence becomes universal, they will be renounced altogether. What is true of the history of one people will be true of the history of another. Religions are not necessary to human progress. They are really clogs. My ancestors had more trouble to extirpate these superstitious ideas from the mind than they had in getting rid of disease and crime. There were several reasons for this difficulty. Disease and crime were self-evident evils, that the narrowest intelligence could perceive; but beliefs in creeds and superstitions were perversions of judgment, resulting from a lack of thorough mental training. As soon, however, as education of a high order became universal, it began to disappear. No mind of philosophical culture can adhere to such superstitions.

"Many ages the people made idols, and, decking them with rich ornaments, placed them in magnificent temples specially built for them and the rites by which they worshipped them. There have existed many variations of this kind of idolatry that are marked by the progressive stages of civilization. Some nations of remote antiquity were highly cultured in art and literature, yet worshipped gods of their own manufacture, or imaginary gods, for everything. Light and darkness, the seasons, earth, air, water, all had a separate deity to preside over and control their special services. They offered sacrifices to these deities as they desired their co-operation or favor in some enterprise to be undertaken.

"In remote antiquity, we read of a great General about to set out upon the sea to attack the army of another nation. In order to propitiate the god of the ocean, he had a fine chariot built to which were harnessed two beautiful white horses. In the presence of a vast concourse of people collected to witness the ceremony, he drove them into the sea. When they sank out of sight it was supposed that the god had accepted the present, and would show his gratitude for it by favoring winds and peaceful weather.

"A thousand years afterward history speaks of the occurrence derisively, as an absurd superstition, and at the same time they believed in and lauded a more absurd and cruel religion. They worshipped an imaginary being who had created and possessed absolute control of everything. Some of the human family it had pleased him to make eminently good, while others he made eminently bad. For those whom he had created with evil desires, he prepared a lake of molten fire into which they were to be cast after death to suffer endless torture for doing what they had been expressly created to do. Those who had been created good were to be rewarded for following out their natural inclinations, by occupying a place near the Deity, where they were to spend eternity in singing praises to him.

"He could, however, be persuaded by prayer from following his original intentions. Very earnest prayer had caused him to change his mind, and send rain when he had previously concluded to visit the country with drouth.

"Two nations at war with each other, and believing in the same Deity, would pray for a pestilence to visit their enemy. Death was universally regarded as a visitation of Providence for some offense committed against him instead of against the laws of nature.

"Some believed that prayer and donations to the church or priest, could induce the Deity to take their relatives from the lake of torment and place them in his own presence. The Deity was prayed to on every occasion, and for every trivial object. The poor and indolent prayed for him to send them food and clothes. The sick prayed for health, the foolish for wisdom, and the revengeful besought the Deity to consign all their enemies to the burning lake.

"The intelligent and humane began to doubt the necessity of such dreadful and needless torment for every conceivable misdemeanor, and it was modified, and eventually dropped altogether. Education finally rooted out every phase of superstition from the minds of the people, and now we look back and smile at the massive and magnificent structures erected to the worship of a Deity who could be coaxed to change his mind by prayer."

I did not tell the Preceptress that she had been giving me a history of my own ancestry; but I remarked the resemblance with the joyous hope that in the future of my own unhappy country lay the possibility of a civilization so glorious, the ideal heaven of which every sorrowing heart had dreamed. But always with the desire to believe it had a spiritual eternity.

CHAPTER IX.

I have described the peculiar ceremony attending the burial of youth in Mizora. Old age, in some respects, had a similar ceremony, but the funeral of an aged person differed greatly from what I had witnessed at the grave of youth. Wauna and I attended the funeral of a very aged lady. Death in Mizora was the gradual failing of mental and physical vigor. It came slowly, and unaccompanied with pain. It was received without regret, and witnessed without tears.

The daughters performed the last labor that the mother required. They arrayed her body for burial and bore it to the grave. If in that season of the year, autumn leaves hid the bier, and formed the covering and pillow of her narrow bed. If not in the fall, full-blown roses and matured flowers were substituted.

The ceremony was conducted by the eldest daughter, assisted by the others. No tears were shed; no mourning worn; no sorrowful chanting. A solemn dirge was sung indicative of decay. A dignified solemnity befitting the farewell to a useful life was manifest in all the proceedings; but no demonstrations of sorrow were visible. The mourners were unveiled, and performed the last services for their mother with calmness. I was so astonished at the absence of mourning that I asked an explanation of Wauna.

"Why should we mourn," was the surprising answer, "for what is inevitable? Death must come, and, in this instance, it came in its natural way. There is nothing to be regretted or mourned over, as there was in the drowning of my young friend. Her life was suddenly arrested while yet in the promise of its fruitfulness. There was cause for grief, and the expressions and emblems of mourning were proper and appropriate. But here, mourning would be out of place, for life has fulfilled its promises. Its work is done, and nature has given the worn-out body rest. That is all."

That sympathy and regret which the city had expressed for the young dead was manifested only in decorum and respectful attendance at the funeral. No one appeared to feel that it was an occasion for mourning. How strange it all seemed to me, and yet there was a philosophy about it that I could not help but admire. Only I wished that they believed as I did, that all of those tender associations would be resumed beyond the grave. If only they could be convinced. I again broached the subject to Wauna. I could not relinquish the hope of converting her to my belief. She was so beautiful, so pure, and I loved her so dearly. I could not give up my hope of an eternal reunion. I appealed to her sympathy.

"What hope," I asked, "can you offer those whose lives have been only successive phases of unhappiness? Why should beings be created only to live a life of suffering, and then die, as many, very many, of my people do? If they had no hope of a spiritual life, where pain and sorrow are to be unknown, the burdens of this life could not be borne."

"You have the same consolation," replied Wauna, "as the Preceptress had in losing her daughter. That daring spirit that cost her her life, was the pride of her mother. She possessed a promising intellect, yet her mother accepts her death as one of the sorrowful phases of life, and bravely tries to subdue its pain. Long ages behind us, as my mother has told you, the history of all human life was but a succession of woes. Our own happy state has been evolved by slow degrees out of that sorrowful past. Human progress is marked by blood and tears, and the heart's bitterest anguish. We, as a people, have progressed almost beyond the reach of sorrow, but you are in the midst of it. You must work for the future, though you cannot be of it."

"I cannot," I declared, "reconcile myself to your belief. I am separated from my child. To think I am never to see it in this world, nor through endless ages, would drive me insane with despair. What consolation can your belief offer *me*?"

"In this life, you may yearn for your child, but after this life you sleep," answered Wauna, sententiously. "And how sweet that sleep! No dreams; no waking to work and trial; no striving after perfection; no planning for the morrow. It is oblivion than which there can be no happier heaven."

"Would not meeting with those you have loved be happier?" I asked, in amazement.

"There would be happiness; and there would be work, too."

"But my religion does not believe in work in heaven," I answered.

"Then it has not taken the immutable laws of Nature into consideration," said Wauna. "If Nature has prepared a conscious existence for us after this body decays, she has prepared work for us, you may rest assured. It might be a grander, nobler work; but it would be work, nevertheless. Then, how restful, in contrast, is our religion. It is eternal, undisturbable rest for both body and brain. Besides, as you say yourself, you cannot be sure of meeting those whom you desire to meet in that other country. They may be the ones condemned to eternal suffering for their sins. Think you I could enjoy myself in any surroundings, when I knew that those who were dear to me in this life, were enduring torment that could have no end. Give me oblivion rather than such a heaven.

"Our punishment comes in this world; but it is not so much through sin as ignorance. The savages lived lives of misery, occasioned by their lack of intelligence. Humanity must always suffer for the mistakes it makes. Misery belongs to the ignorant; happiness to the wise. That is our doctrine of reward and punishment."

"And you believe that my people will one day reject all religions?"

"When they are advanced enough," she answered. "You say you have scholars among you already, who preach their inconsistencies. What do you call them?"

"Philosophers," was my reply.

"They are your prophets," said Wauna. "When they break the shackles that bind you to creeds and dogmas, they will have done much to advance you. To rely on one's own *will* power to do right is the only safe road to morality, and your only heaven."

I left Wauna and sought a secluded spot by the river. I was shocked beyond measure at her confession. It had the earnestness, and, to me, the cruelty of conviction. To live without a spiritual future in anticipation was akin to depravity, to crime and its penalty of prison life forever. Yet here was a people, noble, exalted beyond my conceiving, living in the present, and obeying only a duty to posterity. I recalled a painting I had once seen that always possessed for me a horrible fascination. In a cave, with his foot upon the corpse of a youth, sat the crowned and sceptered majesty of Death. The waters of oblivion encompassed the throne and corpse, which lay with its head and feet bathed in its waters—for out of the Unknown had life come, and to the Unknown had it departed. Before me, in vision, swept the mighty stream of human life from which I had been swept to these strange shores. All its sufferings, its delusions; its baffled struggles; its wrongs, came upon me with a sense of spiritual agony in them that religion—my religion, which was their only consolation—must vanish in the crucible of Science. And that Science was the magician that was to purify and exalt the world. To live in the Present; to die in it and become as the dust; a mere speck, a flash of activity in the far, limitless expanse of Nature, of Force, of Matter in which a spiritual ideal had no part. It was horrible to think of. The prejudices of inherited religious faith, the contracted forces of thought in which I had been born and reared could not be uprooted or expanded without pain.

CHAPTER X.

I had begun to feel an intense longing to return to my own country, but it was accompanied by a desire, equally as strong, to carry back to that woe-burdened land some of the noble lessons and doctrines I had learned in this. I saw no means of doing it that seemed so available as a companion,—a being, born and bred in an atmosphere of honor and grandly humane ideas and actions.

My heart and my judgment turned to Wauna. She was endeared to me by long and gentle association. She was self-reliant and courageous, and possessed a strong will. Who, of all my Mizora acquaints, was so well adapted to the service I required.

When I broached the subject to her, Wauna expressed herself as really pleased with the idea; but when we went to the Preceptress, she acknowledged a strong reluctance to the proposition. She said:

"Wauna can form no conception of the conditions of society in your country. They are far, very far, behind our own. They will, I fear, chafe her own nature more than she can improve theirs. Still, if I thought she could lead your people into a broader intelligence, and start them on the way upward to enlightenment and real happiness, I would let her go. The moment, however, that she desires to return she must be aided to do so."

I pledged myself to abide by any request the Preceptress might make of me. Wauna's own inclinations greatly influenced her mother, and finally we obtained her consent. Our preparations were carefully made. The advanced knowledge of chemistry in Mizora placed many advantages in our way. Our boat was an ingenious contrivance with a thin glass top that could be removed and folded away until needed to protect us from the rigors of the Arctic climate.

I had given an accurate description of the rapids that would oppose us, and our boat was furnished with a motive power sufficient to drive us through them at a higher rate of speed than what they moved at. It was built so as to be easily converted into a sled, and runners were made that could be readily adjusted. We were provided with food and clothing prepared expressly for the severe change to and rigors of the Arctic climate through which we must pass.

I was constantly dreading the terrors of that long ice-bound journey, but the Preceptress appeared to be little concerned about it. When I spoke of its severities, she said for us to observe her directions, and we should not suffer. She asked me if I had ever felt uncomfortable in any of the air-ship voyages I had taken, and said that the cold of the upper regions through which I had passed in their country was quite as intense as any I could meet within a lower atmosphere of my own.

The newspapers had a great deal to say about the departure of the Preceptress' daughter on so uncertain a mission, and to that strange land of barbarians which I represented. When the day arrived for our departure, immense throngs of people from all parts of the country lined the shore, or looked down upon us from their anchored air-ships.

The last words of farewell had been spoken to my many friends and benefactors. Wauna had bidden a multitude of associates good-bye, and clasped her mother's hand, which she held until the boat parted from the shore. Years have passed since that memorable parting, but the look of yearning love in that Mizora mother's eyes haunts me still. Long and vainly has she watched for a boat's prow to cleave that amber mist and bear to her arms that vision of beauty and tender love I took away from her. My heart saddens at the thought of her grief and long, long waiting that only death will end.

We pointed the boat's prow toward the wide mysterious circle of amber mists, and then turned our eyes for a last look at Mizora. Wauna stood silent and calm, earnestly gazing into the eyes of her mother, until the shore and the multitude of fair faces faded like a vision of heaven from our views.

"O beautiful Mizora!" cried the voice of my heart. "Shall I ever again see a land so fair, where natures so noble and aims so lofty have their abiding place? Memory will return to you though my feet may never again tread your delightful shores. Farewell, sweet ideal land of my Soul, of Humanity, farewell!"

My thoughts turned to that other world from which I had journeyed so long. Would the time ever come when it, too, would be a land of universal intelligence and happiness? When the difference of nations would be settled by argument instead of battle? When disease, deformity and premature death would be unknown? When locks, and bolts and bars would be useless?

I hoped so much from the personal influence of Wauna. So noble, so utterly unconscious of wrong, she must surely revolutionize human nature whenever it came in contact with her own.

I pictured to myself my own dear land—dear, despite its many phases of wretchedness—smiling in universal comfort and health. I imagined its political prisons yawning with emptiness, while their haggard and decrepit and sorrowful occupants hobbled out into the sunshine of liberty, and the new life we were bringing to them. Fancy flew abroad on the wings of hope, dropping the seeds of progress wherever it passed.

The poor should be given work, and justly paid for it, instead of being supported by charity. The charity that had fostered indolence in its mistaken efforts to do good, should be employed to train poverty to skillful labor and economy in living. And what a world of good that one measure would produce! The poor should possess exactly the same educational advantages that were supplied to the rich. In this *one* measure, if I could only make it popular, I would see the golden promise of the future of my country. "Educate your poor and they will work out their own salvation. Educated Labor can dictate its rights to Capital."

How easy of accomplishment it all seemed to me, who had seen the practical benefits arising to a commonwealth that had adopted these mottoes. I doubted not that the wiser and better of my own people would aid and encourage me. Free education would lead to other results.

Riches should be accumulated only by vast and generous industries that reached a helping hand to thousands of industrious poor, instead of grinding them out of a few hundred of poorly-paid and over-worked artisans. Education in the hands of the poor would be a powerful agent with which they would alleviate their own condition, and defend themselves against oppression and knavery.

The prisons should be supplied with schools as well as work-rooms, where the intellect should be trained and cultivated, and where moral idiocy, by the stern and rigorous law of Justice to Innocence, should be forced to deny itself posterity.

No philanthropical mind ever spread the wings of its fancy for a broader flight.

CHAPTER XI.

Our journey was a perilous one with all our precautions. The passage through the swiftest part of the current almost swamped our boat. The current that opposed us was so strong, that when we increased our speed our boat appeared to be cleaving its way through a wall of waters. Wauna was perfectly calm, and managed the motor with the steadiest nerves. Her courage inspired me, though many a time I despaired of ever getting out of the rapids. When we did, and looked up at the star-gemmed canopy that stretches above my own world, and abroad over the dark and desolate waste of waters around us, it gave me an impression of solemn and weird magnificence. It was such a contrast to the vivid nights of Mizora, to which my eyes had so long been accustomed, that it came upon me like a new scene.

The stars were a source of wonder and ceaseless delight to Wauna. "It looks," she said, "as though a prodigal hand had strewn the top of the atmosphere with diamonds."

The journey over fields of ice and snow was monotonous, but, owing to the skill and knowledge of Mizora displayed in our accoutrements, it was deprived of its severities. The wind whistled past us without any other greeting than its melancholy sound. We looked out from our snug quarters on the dismal hills of snow and ice without a sensation of distress. The Aurora Borealis hung out its streamers of beauty, but they were pale compared to what Wauna had seen in her own country. The Esquimaux she presumed were animals.

We traveled far enough south to secure passage upon a trading-vessel bound for civilized shores. The sun came up with his glance of fire and his banners of light, laying his glorious touch on cloud and water, and kissing the cheek with his warmth. He beamed upon us from the zenith, and sank behind the western clouds with a lingering glance of beauty. The moon came up like the ghost of the sun, casting a weird yet tender beauty on every object. To Wauna it was a revelation of magnificence in nature beyond her contriving.

"How grand," she exclaimed, "are the revelations of nature in your world! To look upon them, it seems to me, would broaden and deepen the mind with the very vastness of their splendor. Nature has been more bountiful to you than to Mizora. The day with its heart of fire, and the night with its pale beauty are grander than ours. They speak of vast and incomprehensible power."

When I took Wauna to the observatory, and she looked upon the countless multitudes of worlds and suns revolving in space so far away that a sun and its satellites looked like a ball of mist, she said that words could not describe her sensations.

"To us," she said, "the leaves of Nature's book are the winds and waves, the bud and bloom and decay of seasons. But here every leaf is a world. A mighty hand has sprinkled the suns like fruitful seeds across the limitless fields of space. Can human nature contemplate a scene so grand that reaches so far beyond the grasp of mind, and not feel its own insignificance, and the littleness of selfish actions? And yet you can behold these myriads of worlds and systems of worlds wheeling in the dim infinity of space—a spectacle awful in its vastness—and turn to the practice of narrow superstitions?"

At last the shores of my native land greeted my longing eyes, and the familiar scenes of my childhood drew near. But when, after nearly twenty years absence, I stood on the once familiar spot, the graves of my heart's dear ones were all that was mine. My little one had died soon after my exile. My father had soon followed. Suspected, and finally persecuted by the government, my husband had fled the country, and, nearly as I could discover, had sought that universal asylum for the oppressed of all nations—the United States. And thither I turned my steps.

In my own country and in France, the friends who had known me in girlhood were surprised at my youthful appearance. I did not explain the cause of it to them, nor did I mention the people or country from whence I had come. Wauna was my friend and a foreigner—that was all.

The impression she made was all that I had anticipated. Her unusual beauty and her evident purity attracted attention wherever she went. The wonderful melody of her singing was much commented upon, but in Mizora she had been considered but an indifferent singer. But I had made a mistake in my anticipation of her personal influence. The gentleness and delicacy of her character received the tenderest respect. None who looked upon that face or met the glance of the dark soft eyes ever doubted that the nature that animated them was pure and beautiful. Yet it was the respect felt for a character so exceptionably superior that imitation and emulation would be impossible.

"She is too far above the common run of human nature," said one observer. "I should not be surprised if her spirit were already pluming its wings for a heavenly flight. Such natures never stay long among us."

The remark struck my heart with a chill of depression. I looked at Wauna and wondered why I had noticed sooner the shrinking outlines of the once round cheek. Too gentle to show disgust, too noble to ill-treat, the spirit of Wauna was chafing under the trying associations. Men and women alike regarded her as an impossible character, and I began to realize with a sickening regret that I had made a mistake. In my own country, in France and England, her beauty was her sole attraction to men. The lofty ideal of humanity that she represented was smiled at or gently ignored.

"The world would be a paradise," said one philosopher, "if such characters were common. But one is like a seed in the ocean; it cannot do much good."

When we arrived in the United States, its activity and evident progress impressed Wauna with a feeling more nearly akin to companionship. Her own character received a juster appreciation.

"The time is near," she said, "when the New World will be the teacher of the Old in the great lesson of Humanity. You will live to see it demonstrate to the world the justice and policy of giving to every child born under its flag the highest mental, moral and physical training known to the present age. You can hardly realize what twenty-five years of free education will bring to it. They are already on the right path, but they are still many centuries behind my own country in civilization, in their government and modes of dispensing justice. Yet their free schools, as yet imperfect, are, nevertheless, fruitful seeds of progress."

Yet here the nature of Wauna grew restless and homesick, and she at last gave expression to her longing for home.

"I am not suited to your world," she said, with a look of deep sorrow in her lovely eyes. "None of my people are. We are too finely organized. I cannot look with any degree of calmness upon the practices of your civilization. It is a common thing to see mothers ill-treat their own helpless little ones. The pitiful cries of the children keep ringing in my ears. Cannot mothers realize that they are whipping a mean spirit into their offspring instead of out. I have heard the most enlightened deny their own statements when selfishness demanded it. I cannot mention the half of the things I witness daily that grates upon my feelings. I cannot reform them. It is not for such as I to be a reformer. Those who need reform are the ones to work for it."

Sorrowfully I bade adieu to my hopes and my search for Alexis, and prepared to accompany Wauna's return. We embarked on a whaling vessel, and having reached its farthest limit, we started on our perilous journey north; perilous for the lack of our boat, of which we could hear nothing. It had been left in charge of a party of Esquimaux, and had either been destroyed, or was hidden. Our progress, therefore, depended entirely upon the Esquimaux. The tribe I had journeyed so far north with had departed, and those whom I solicited to accompany us professed to be ignorant of the sea I mentioned. Like all low natures, the Esquimaux are intensely selfish. Nothing could induce them to assist us but the most apparent benefit to themselves; and this I could not assure them. The homesickness, and coarse diet and savage surroundings told rapidly on the sensitive nature of Wauna. In a miserable Esquimaux hut, on a pile of furs, I saw the flame of a beautiful and grandly noble life die out. My efforts were hopeless; my anguish keen. O Humanity, what have I sacrificed for you!

"Oh, Wauna," I pleaded, as I saw the signs of dissolution approaching, "shall I not pray for you?"

"Prayers cannot avail me," she replied, as her thin hands reached and closed over one of mine. "I had hoped once more to see the majestic hills and smiling valleys of my own sweet land, but I shall not. If I could only go to sleep in the arms of my mother. But the Great Mother of us all will soon receive me in her bosom. And oh! my friend, promise me that her dust shall cover me from the sight of men. When my mother rocked me to slumber on her bosom, and soothed me with her gentle lullaby, she little dreamed that I should suffer and die first. If you ever reach Mizora, tell her only that I sleep the sleep of oblivion. She will know. Let the memory of my suffering die with me."

"Oh, Wauna," I exclaimed, in anguish, "you surely have a soul. How can anything so young, so pure, so beautiful, be doomed to annihilation?"

"We are not annihilated," was the calm reply. "And as to beauty, are the roses not beautiful? Yet they die and you say it is the end of the year's roses. The birds are harmless, and their songs make the woods melodious with the joy of life, yet they die, and you say they have no after life. We are like the roses, but our lives are for a century and more. And when our lives are ended, the Great Mother gathers us in. We are the harvest of the centuries."

When the dull, gray light of the Arctic morning broke, it fell gently upon the presence of Death.

With the assistance of the Esquimaux, a grave was dug, and a rude wooden cross erected on which I wrote the one word "Wauna," which, in the language of Mizora, means "Happiness."

The world to which I have returned is many ages behind the civilization of Mizora.

Though we cannot hope to attain their perfection in our generation, yet many, very many, evils could be obliterated were we to follow their laws. Crime is as hereditary as disease.

No savant now denies the transmittable taint of insanity and consumption. There are some people in the world now, who, knowing the possibility of afflicting offspring with hereditary disease, have lived in ascetic celibacy. But where do we find a criminal who denies himself offspring, lest he endow posterity with the horrible capacity for murder that lies in his blood?

The good, the just, the noble, close heart and eyes to the sweet allurements of domestic life, lest posterity suffer physically or mentally by them. But the criminal has no restraints but what the law enforces. Ignorance, poverty and disease, huddled in dens of wretchedness, where they multiply with reckless improvidence, sometimes fostered by mistaken charity.

The future of the world, if it be grand and noble, will be the result of UNIVERSAL EDUCATION, FREE AS THE GOD-GIVEN WATER WE DRINK.

In the United States I await the issue of universal liberty. In this refuge for oppression, my husband found a grave. Childless, homeless and friendless, in poverty and obscurity, I have written the story of my wanderings. The world's fame can never warm a heart already dead to happiness; but out of the agony of one human life, may come a lesson for many. Life is a tragedy even under the most favorable conditions.

THE END

Lightning Source UK Ltd.
Milton Keynes UK
UKHW041405280119
336340UK00001B/92/P